Acclaim for Yu Hua's

China in Ten Words

人民 领袖 阅读 写作 鲁迅 革命 差距 草根 山寨 忽悠

"This is a tale told by a raconteur, not an academic. . . . The most powerful and vivid sections reach back to Yu Hua's childhood during the Cultural Revolution. . . . It is a cautionary tale about the risks of subterfuge, of trying to sneak something past one's father—or, perhaps, one's ever vigilant government." —*The New York Times Book Review*

"A panoramic view, elegantly distilled. I wish I had—and remotely could have—done it. Yu Hua writes with humor and anger, and, unlike much of the zeitgeist writing that describes and defines this moment in China, this book works in English extremely well." —Evan Osnos, *The New Yorker*

"If Yu Hua never wrote anything else, he would rate entry into the pantheon of greats for 'Reading,' an essay in his new collection *China in Ten Words*. Nothing I've ever read captures both the power and subversive nature of youthful reading as well. . . . For American readers curious about the upheavals of China, this may be the right moment to discover Yu Hua." —Jim Higgins, *Milwaukee Journal Sentinel*

"At times humorous, at times heartbreaking, and at times fierce, these ten moving and informative essays form a small kaleidoscopic view of contemporary China. . . . Written with a novelist's eye and narrative flair, *China in Ten Words* will make the reader rethink 'the China miracle.'"
—Ha Jin, National Book
Award–winning author of *Waiting*

"It's rare to find a work of fiction that can be hysterically funny at some points, while deeply moving and disturbing at others. It's even more unusual to find such qualities in a work of nonfiction. But *China in Ten Words* is just such an extraordinary work." —Los Angeles Review of Books.com

"A collection of ten quietly audacious essays that blend memoir with social commentary. . . . . The insight it offers and the force and authority it packs is of a kind that few, if any, of those louder, more attention-seeking must-read books can even pretend to match."   —*The National Post*

"A discursively simple series of essays explaining his country's recent history through ten central terms. . . . Caustic and difficult to forget, *China in Ten Words* is a people's-eye view of a world in which the people have little place."
—Pico Iyer, *Time* (Asia)

"One of China's most prominent writers. . . . In his sublime essay collection, Hua explores his often spartan childhood during the Cultural Revolution in the 1960s and 1970s and the rampant corruption of modern China."
—*The Star-Ledger* (Newark)

"In this era of the China Boom, when Communist Party officials are so inclined to erase the travails of their country's past from public consciousness, Yu Hua's insistence on 'remembering' comes as an almost shocking intrusion into a willful state of amnesia. His earthy, even ribald, meditations on growing up in small-town China during Mao's Cultural Revolution remind us of just how twisted China's progress into the present has been and how precariously balanced its success story actually still is."
—Orville Schell, Director of the Center
on U.S.–China Relations, The Asia Society

YU HUA

China in Ten Words

人民 领袖 阅读 写作 鲁迅 革命 差距 草根 山寨 忽悠

Yu Hua is the author of four novels, six collections of stories, and three collections of essays. His work has been translated into more than twenty languages. In 2002, he became the first Chinese writer to win the James Joyce Award. His novel *Brothers* was shortlisted for the Man Asian Literary Prize and awarded France's Prix Courrier International. *To Live* was awarded Italy's Premio Grinzane Cavour, and *To Live* and *Chronicle of a Blood Merchant* were ranked among the ten most influential books in China in the 1990s by *Wen Hui Bao*, the largest newspaper in Shanghai. Yu Hua lives in Beijing.

Also by Yu Hua

Brothers

Cries in the Drizzle

Chronicle of a Blood Merchant

To Live

The Past and the Punishments

China in Ten Words

人民
people

领袖
leader

阅读
reading

写作
writing

鲁迅
lu xun

革命
revolution

差距
disparity

草根
grassroots

山寨
copycat

忽悠
bamboozle

China
in
Ten
Words

YU HUA

Translated
from the Chinese
by Allan H. Barr

ANCHOR BOOKS

A DIVISION OF RANDOM HOUSE, INC.

NEW YORK

FIRST ANCHOR BOOKS EDITION, AUGUST 2012

Translation copyright © 2011 by Yu Hua

All rights reserved. Published in the United States by
Anchor Books, a division of Random House, Inc., New York,
and in Canada by Random House of Canada Limited, Toronto. This
work, originally written in Chinese, was first published in France
as *La Chine en Dix Mots* by Actes Sud, Arles, France, in 2010.
French translation copyright © 2010 by Actes Sud. A Chinese edition
of this work was published in Taiwan as *Shige cihui li de Zhongguo* by
Rye Field Publications, Taipei, in 2011. Copyright © 2011 by Yu Hua. This
translation originally published in hardcover in the United States by
Pantheon Books, a division of Random House, Inc., New York, in 2011.

A portion of this work was originally published in
different form in *The New York Times*.

The Library of Congress has cataloged the
Pantheon Books edition as follows:
Yu, Hua.
[Shige cihui li zhong de zhongguo. English]
China in ten words / Yu Hua ; translated from the Chinese by Allan H.
Barr.
p. cm.
I. Barr, Allan Hepburn. II. Title.
PL2928.H78S5513 2011
985.1'85207—dc22 2011010320

Anchor ISBN: 978-0-307-73979-7

Author photograph courtesy of Fabrica
Book design by Iris Weinstein

www.anchorbooks.com

Printed in the United States of America
15   14   13

contents

introduction

In 1978 I got my first job—as a small-town dentist in south China. This mostly involved pulling teeth, but as the youngest staff member I was given another task as well. Every summer, with a straw hat on my head and a medical case on my back, I would shuttle back and forth between the town's factories and kindergartens, administering vaccinations to workers and children.

China during the Mao era was a poor country, but it had a strong public health network that provided free immunizations to its citizens. That was where I came in. In those days there were no disposable needles and syringes; we had to reuse ours again and again. Sterilization too was primitive: The needles and syringes would be washed, wrapped separately in gauze, and placed in aluminum lunch boxes laid in a large wok on top of a briquette stove. Water was added to the wok, and the needles and syringes were then steamed for two hours, as you would steam buns.

On my first day of giving injections I went to a factory. The workers rolled up their sleeves and waited in line, baring their arms to me one after another—and offering up a tiny piece of red flesh, too. Because the needles had been used multiple times, almost every one of them had a barbed tip. You could stick a needle into someone's arm easily enough, but when you extracted it, you would pull out a tiny piece of flesh along with it. For the workers the pain was bearable, although they would grit their teeth or perhaps let out a groan or two. I paid them no mind, for the workers had had to put up with barbed needles year after year and should be used to it by now, I thought. But the next day, when I went to a kindergarten to give shots to children from the ages of three through six, it was a different story. Every last one of them burst out weeping and wailing. Because their skin was so tender, the needles would snag bigger shreds of flesh than they had from the workers, and the children's wounds bled more profusely. I still remember how the children were all sobbing uncontrollably; the ones who had yet to be inoculated were crying even louder than those who had already had their shots. The pain that the children saw others suffering, it seemed to me, affected them even more intensely than the pain they themselves experienced, because it made their fear all the more acute.

This scene left me shocked and shaken. When I got back to the hospital, I did not clean the instruments right away. Instead, I got hold of a grindstone and ground all the needles until they were completely straight and the points were sharp. But these old needles were so prone to metal fatigue that after two or three more uses they would acquire barbs again, so grinding the needles became a regular part of my routine, and the more I sharpened, the shorter they got. That summer it was always dark by the time I left the hospital, with fingers blistered by my labors at the grindstone.

Later, whenever I recalled this episode, I was guilt-stricken that I'd had to see the children's reaction to realize how much the factory workers must have suffered. If, before I had given shots to others, I had pricked my own arm with a barbed needle and pulled out a blood-stained shred of my own flesh, then I would have known how painful it was long before I heard the children's wails.

This remorse left a profound mark, and it has stayed with me through all my years as an author. It is when the suffering of others becomes part of my own experience that I truly know what it is to live and what it is to write. Nothing in the world, perhaps, is so likely to forge a connection between people as pain, because the connection that comes from that source comes from deep in the heart. So when in this book I write of China's pain, I am registering my pain too, because China's pain is mine.

The arrow hits the target, leaving the string," Dante wrote, and by inverting cause and effect he impresses on us how quickly an action can happen. In China's breathtaking changes during the past thirty years we likewise find a pattern of development where the relationship between cause and effect is turned on its head. Practically every day we find ourselves surrounded by consequences, but seldom do we trace these outcomes back to their roots. The result is that conflicts and problems—which have sprouted everywhere like weeds during these past decades—are concealed amid the complacency generated by our rapid economic advances. My task here is to reverse normal procedure: to start from the effects that seem so glorious and search for their causes, whatever discomfort that may entail.

"We survive in adversity and perish in ease and comfort."* Such were the words of the Confucian philosopher Mencius, citing six worthies in antiquity who suffered untold hardship before achieving greatness. Man is bound to make mistakes, he believed, and it is in the unceasing correction of his errors that human progress lies. Viewed in this light, he suggested, adversity has a way of enhancing our endurance, while ease and comfort tend to hasten

*Mencius, trans. D. C. Lau (Harmondsworth, U.K.: Penguin Books, 1970), p. 181.

our demise—whether as individuals or as a nation. When I write in these pages of personal pain and of China's pain, it is with that same conviction that we survive in adversity. So in this quest to follow things back to their source, we cannot help but stumble upon one misfortune after another.

If I were to try to attend to each and every aspect of modern China, there would be no end to this endeavor, and the book would go on longer than *The Thousand and One Nights*. So I limit myself to just ten words. But this tiny lexicon gives me ten pairs of eyes with which to scan the contemporary Chinese scene from different vantage points.

My aim is to stay brief and concise, beginning this narrative journey from the daily life we know so well. Daily life may seem trivial and routine, but in fact it contains a multitude of incidents, at once rich, expansive, and touching. Politics, history, society, and culture, one's memories and emotions, desires and secrets—all reverberate there. Daily life is a veritable forest and, as the Chinese saying goes, "Where woods grow deep, you'll find every kind of bird."

For me, as for a bus driver who drives back and forth along the same route, my starting point is also my last stop. My busload of stories sets off from daily life, pulls over when it reaches junctions with politics, history, society, and culture—or with memories and emotions, desires and secrets—and sometimes it pauses at outlying stops that may not even have a name. Some stories disembark along the way, while others board; and eventually, after all this bustle to and fro, my bus returns to where it started.

My goal, then, is to compress the endless chatter of China today into ten simple words; to bring together observation, analysis, and personal anecdote in a narrative that roams freely across time and space; and finally to clear a path through the social complexities and staggering contrasts of contemporary China.

China in Ten Words

人民

people

As I write these characters I have to look a second time to make sure I have them right. That's the thing about this word: it feels remote, but it's so familiar, too.

I can't think of another expression in the modern Chinese language that is such an anomaly—ubiquitous yet somehow invisible. In China today it's only officials who have "the people"* on their lips every time they open their mouths, for the people themselves seldom use the term—perhaps they hardly recall its existence. We have to give those voluble officials some credit, for we rely on them to demonstrate that the phrase still has some currency.

In the past this was such a weighty phrase. Our country was called the People's Republic of China. Chairman Mao told us to "serve the people." The most important paper was the *People's Daily*. "Since 1949 the people are the masters," we learned to say.

In my childhood years "the people" was just as marvelous an expression as "Chairman Mao," and when I first began to read, these were the first words I mastered; I could write them even before I could write my own name or the names

---

*In Pinyin romanization, *renmin*

of my parents. It was my view then that "the people are Chairman Mao, and Chairman Mao is the people."

That was during the Cultural Revolution, and I marched about proudly sharing this insight with everyone I met. They responded with dubious looks, apparently finding something problematic about my formulation, although nobody directly contradicted me. In those days people walked on eggshells, fearful that if they said anything wrong, they might be branded a counterrevolutionary, endangering their whole family. My parents, hearing of my discovery, looked equally doubtful. They eyed me warily and told me in a roundabout way that they couldn't see anything wrong with what I'd said but I still had better not say it again.

But since this was my greatest childhood insight, I couldn't bear to hush it up and continued sharing it with the world at large. One day I found supporting evidence in a popular saying of the time, "Chairman Mao lives in our hearts." I took this to its logical conclusion: "Chairman Mao lives in everyone's heart, so what lives in Chairman Mao's heart? It has to be the entire people." Therefore: "The people are Chairman Mao, and Chairman Mao is the people."

Those doubtful looks among the residents of my little town gradually dissipated. Some people began nodding in approval, and others began to say the same thing—my little playmates first, and then grown-ups, too.

But I felt threatened when lots of people started saying, "The people are Chairman Mao, and Chairman Mao is the people." In a revolutionary era one cannot claim a patent for anything, and I found my status as inventor was being steadily eroded. "I was the first one to say that," I would declare. But no adults set any store by my claim of authorship, and in the end even my young companions refused to accept that I deserved credit. Faced with my strenuous arguments or pathetic pleas, they would shake their heads: "No, everybody says that."

I was upset, regretting bitterly that I had made my discovery public. I should have stored it forever in my own mind, safe from anybody else, keeping it for myself to savor my whole life through.

These days the West is astonished by the speed of China's makeover. With the flick of a wrist Chinese history has utterly changed its complexion, much the way an actor in Sichuan opera swaps one mask for another. In the short space of thirty years, a China ruled by politics has transformed itself into a China where money is king.

Turning points in history tend to be marked by some emblematic event, and the Tiananmen Incident of 1989 was one such moment. Stirred by the death that April of the reform-minded Hu Yaobang, college students in Beijing poured out of their campuses to gather in Tiananmen Square, demanding democratic freedoms and denouncing official corruption. Because of the hard line the government took in refusing to engage in a dialogue, in mid-May the students began a hunger strike in the square and the locals marched in the streets to support them. Beijing residents were actually not so interested in "democratic freedoms"—it was the attacks on profiteering by officials that drew them into the movement in such huge numbers. At that time Deng Xiaoping's open-door policy had entered its eleventh year, and although the reforms had triggered price increases, the economy was growing steadily and the standard of living was rising. Peasants had benefited from the changes. Factories had yet to close, and workers were yet to become victims. Contradictions were not as acute then as they are now, when society simmers with rage. All we heard then were grumbles and complaints about the way the children of high officials had made themselves rich on our national resources, and those sentiments found a focus in the protests. Compared with today's large-scale, multifarious corruption, the diversion of funds by a minority back then didn't really amount to anything. Since 1990, corruption has grown with the same astounding speed as the economy as a whole.

The mass movement that had begun to sweep across the country quickly subsided amid the gunfire on the morning of June 4. In October of that year, when I visited Peking University, I found myself in a different world, where engagement with affairs of state was nowhere to be found. After nightfall, courting couples appeared by the lakeside and the clatter of mahjong tiles and the drone of English words being memorized were the only sounds that wafted from dorm windows. In the short space of one summer everything had changed so much that it seemed as though nothing at all had happened that spring. Such a huge contrast demonstrated one point: that the political passions that had erupted in Tiananmen—political passions that had accumulated since the Cultural Revolution—had finally expended themselves completely in one fell swoop, to be replaced by a passion for getting rich. When everyone united in the urge to make money, the economic surge of the 1990s was the natural outcome.

After that, new vocabulary started sprouting up everywhere—netizens, stock traders, fund holders, celebrity fans, laid-off workers, migrant laborers, and so on—slicing into smaller pieces the already faded concept that was "the people." During the Cultural Revolution, the definition of "the people" could not have been simpler, namely "workers, peasants, soldiers, scholars, merchants"—"merchants" meaning not businessmen but, rather, those employed in commercial ventures, like shop clerks. Tiananmen, you could say, marked the watershed between two different conceptions of "the people"; or, to put it another way, it conducted an asset reshuffle, stripping away the original content and replacing it with something new.

In the forty-odd years from the start of the Cultural Revolution to the present, the expression "the people" has been denuded of meaning by Chinese realities. To use a current buzzword, "the people" has become nothing more than a shell company, utilized by different eras to position different products in the marketplace.

Beijing in the spring of 1989 was anarchist heaven. The police suddenly disappeared from the streets, and students and locals took on police duties in their place. It was a Beijing we are unlikely to see again. A common purpose and shared aspirations put a police-free city in perfect order. As you walked down the street you felt a warm, friendly atmosphere all around you. You could take the subway or a bus for free, and everyone was smiling at one another, barriers down. We no longer witnessed arguments in the street. Hard-nosed street vendors were now handing out free refreshments to the protestors. Retirees would withdraw cash from their meager bank savings and make donations to the hunger strikers in the square. Even pickpockets issued a declaration in the name of the Thieves' Association: as a show of support for the students, they were calling a moratorium on all forms of theft. Beijing then was a city where, you could say, "all men are brothers."

If you live in a Chinese city, there's one feeling you never shake off: what a lot of people there are! But it was only with the mass protests in Tiananmen Square that it really came home to you: China is the world's most populous nation. Every day the Square was a sea of people. Students who had poured into Beijing from other parts of the country would stand in the square or on a street corner, giving speeches day after day until their throats grew hoarse and they lost their voices. Their audience—whether wizened old men or mothers with babies in their arms—greeted the speakers with respect, nodding repeatedly and applauding warmly, however immature the students' faces or naive their views.

There were comical moments, too. One afternoon I took my place in a dimly lit conference room in the Chinese Academy of Social Sciences for a meeting of the Capital Intellectual Coalition, a newly formed association of liberal intellectuals in Beijing. As we awaited the arrival of a prominent political scientist named Yan Jiaqi I noticed that some people were taking a newspaper editor to task. His paper had just published a statement by the coalition, and these people were unhappy because their names were low on the list of signatories, beneath the names of less well-known individuals. Why had these nobodies been given a higher ranking? The hapless editor said it wasn't his fault but apologized anyway, nevertheless failing to mollify his critics. This farcical episode came to an end only with the arrival of Yan Jiaqi.

I remember the moment clearly; it was the first and last time I saw him. This distinguished scholar—a close associate of Zhao Ziyang, the general secretary of the Communist Party, who favored a conciliatory line toward the demonstrators—walked in with a somber expression on his face. People quieted down as he delivered a piece of bad news. "Ziyang is in the hospital," he said in a low voice.

In the political context of 1989, for a government leader to be hospitalized could mean only that he had lost power or that he had gone into hiding. Everyone immediately understood the implications. Some began to slip away quietly, and soon they had scattered far and wide, like falling leaves in an autumn gale.

After Tiananmen Zhao Ziyang disappeared from view, and nothing more was heard of him until his death in 2005. Only then did the New China News Agency issue a brief statement: "Comrade Zhao had long suffered from multiple diseases affecting his respiratory and cardiovascular systems, and had been hospitalized for medical treatment on multiple occasions. In recent days his condition deteriorated, and efforts to revive him proved unsuccessful. He died in Beijing on January 17, aged 85."

In China, even if it's just a retired minister who dies, the official announcement will usually be a lot more detailed than this. The statement said nothing about the career of a man who had once been leader of the party and the nation, nor did it mention the date of his memorial service. But word leaked out to a group of petitioners—or "judicial refugees," as they have come to be known—who lived in Beijing South Station. I have no idea through what channels these most disadvantaged of all "people" in China got hold of this information, but they organized themselves and went off to pay their final respects to Zhao Ziyang. They were not authorized to attend, so the police naturally blocked them from entering, but they unfurled a commemorative inscription all the same.

These petitioners had sought legal redress for injustice and oppression in their home districts, only to find themselves stymied at every turn by bias and corruption in the judicial system. China's extralegal appeals procedure—a remnant of its hallowed tradition of humane government—offers a slender hope that some honest official might dispense justice where law has failed. Petitioners exhaust all their resources as they roam from place to place in search of a fair-minded administrator, and ultimately they make their way to Beijing in the hope that someone in the central government will respond to their pleas. In 2004 the official total of such cases reached 10 million. Their desperate plight almost defies imagination: fighting hunger, they sleep in the streets, only to be harried by the police, driven like beggars hither and yon, and written off by some well-heeled intellectuals as mentally deranged. It was precisely such "people" who went to bid farewell to Zhao Ziyang in January 2005. They felt

that he was "the biggest fall guy in China," a bigger victim
of injustice than even they themselves. However much they
had suffered, they at least had a chance to petition, but Zhao
Ziyang, they said, "had nowhere to take his complaint."

I made a trip back to my home in Zhejiang at the end of
May 1989, and after I'd attended to family affairs, I boarded
the train back to Beijing on the afternoon of June 3. I lay
on my bunk listening to the rumble of the wheels on the
tracks; when lights came on in the compartment, I knew
that night was falling. At that moment the student protests
seemed as long and protracted as a marathon, and I could
not imagine when they would end. But when I woke in the
early morning, the train was approaching Beijing and the
news was coming over the radio that the army was now in
Tiananmen Square.

After the gunfire on June 4, the students—from Beijing
and from out of town—began to abandon the city. I vividly
recall the surging throngs filling the station that morning:
just as people were fleeing the capital in droves, I was making an ill-timed reentry. With my bag over my shoulder I
stumbled, dazed, into the station plaza. As I collided with
people swarming in from the other direction, I realized I
would soon be doing exactly the same thing.

When I left again on June 7, service between Beijing and
Shanghai had been suspended because a train in Shanghai
had been set on fire, so my plan was to take a roundabout
route: by train to Wuhan and by boat from there to Zhejiang. Some classmates and I hired a flatbed-cart driver to
take us down Chang'an Avenue to the railroad station. Beijing, seething with activity a few days earlier, now looked
desolate and abandoned. There was hardly a pedestrian
to be seen, only smoke rising from some charred vehicles
and a tank stationed at the Jianguomen overpass, its bar-
rel pointing at us menacingly as we crossed. After pushing
our way through the scrum outside the ticket office, we

finally managed to buy tickets, though it was impossible to reserve seats. As we entered the station we were scrutinized minutely by the soldiers on duty; I was waved in only when they were sure I didn't look like any of the fugitives whose photos appeared on their wanted list.

Never before or since have I traveled on such a crowded train. The compartment was filled with college students fleeing the capital, and everyone was so crammed together there was not an inch of space between one person and the next. An hour out of Beijing, I needed to use the toilet. It took all my strength to squeeze any distance through the throng, and before I was halfway there I realized that my cause was hopeless. I could hear someone yelling and banging on the door, but the toilet itself was full of people—"We can't open it!" they shouted back. I just had to hold on for the full three hours until we got to Shijiazhuang. There I disembarked and found a toilet, then a pay phone, to appeal for help from the editor of the local literary magazine. "Everything's in such chaos now," he said after hearing me out. "Just give up on the idea of going anywhere else. Stay here and write us a story."

So I spent the next month holed up in Shijiazhuang, but I had a hard time writing. Every day the television broadcast shots of students on the wanted list being taken into custody, and these pictures were repeated again and again in rolling coverage—something I've never seen since, except when Chinese athletes have won gold medals in the Olympics. Far from home, in my cheerless hotel room, I saw the despairing looks on the faces of the captured students and heard the crowing of the news announcers, and a chill went down my spine.

Suddenly one day the picture on my TV screen changed completely. Gone were the shots of detained suspects, and gone was the jubilant commentary. Although manhunts and arrests carried on as before, broadcasts now reverted to the old familiar formula: scenes of prosperity throughout the motherland. A day earlier the announcer had been passionately denouncing the crimes of the captured students, and now he was cheerfully lauding our nation's thriving progress. From that day on, just as Zhao Ziyang disappeared from view, so too Tiananmen vanished from the Chinese media. I never saw the slightest mention of it afterward, as though it had never happened. And memories seemed to fade even among those who took part in the protests of spring 1989; the pressures of life, perhaps, allowed little room to revisit the past. Twenty years later, it is a disturbing fact that among the younger generation in China today few know anything about the Tiananmen Incident, and those who do say vaguely, "A lot of people in the streets then, that's what I heard."

Twenty years may have gone by in a flash, but historical memory, I am certain, does not slip away so quickly. No matter how they currently view the events of 1989, I think everyone who participated in them will find those experiences etched indelibly profoundly in their minds when one day they have occasion to look back at that chapter of their lives.

In my case, the thing that has left the deepest mark on me is a realization of what "the people" means.

Sometimes one needs an opportunity to truly encounter a certain word. We encounter all kinds of words in the course of our lives, and some we understand at first glance and others we may rub shoulders with but never fully understand. "The people" belongs in that second category. It's one of the first phrases I learned to read and write, and it has clung to me in my travels through life, constantly appearing before my eyes and sounding in my ears. But it did not truly penetrate my inner being until my thirtieth year, when an experience late one night finally allowed me to understand the term in all its potency. It was only when I had a real-life encounter with it—disengaged from all linguistic, socio-logical, or anthropological theories and definitions—that I could tell myself: "the people" is not an empty phrase, because I have seen it in the flesh, its heart thumping.

It was not the enormous rallies in Tiananmen Square that imparted this understanding, but an episode in another part of town one night in late May 1989. Martial law had been declared by that time; students and residents alike gathered spontaneously to defend every major intersection in Beijing as well as all overpasses and subway exits, to block armed troops from entering Tiananmen Square.

I was then studying at the Lu Xun Literary Institute in Shilipu, on the east side of the city. Practically every lunch-time I would ride my rickety old bike to Tiananmen Square, lingering there through the evening and into the early hours, when I would cycle back to the institute.

Beijing in May can be hot at midday but cold at night. I remember I was wearing only a short-sleeved shirt when I set off after lunch, and by late that evening I was chilled to the bone. As I cycled back from the square an icy wind blew in my face, making every part of me shiver—and every part of my bicycle, too. The streetlights were dark, and only the moon pointed the way ahead. The farther I rode, the colder I felt. But as I approached Hujialou, a current of warm air suddenly swept over me, and it only got warmer as I rode on. I heard a song drifting my way, and a bit later I saw lights gleaming in the distance. Then an astonishing scene appeared before me. Now bathed in warmth, I could see the intersection flooded with light; ten thousand people must have been standing guard on the bridge and the approach roads beneath. They were fervid with passion, lustily sing-ing the national anthem under the night sky: "With our flesh and blood we will build a new great wall! The Chinese people have reached the critical hour, compelled to give their final call! Arise, arise, arise! United we stand. . . ."

Although unarmed, they stood steadfast, confident that with their bodies alone they could block soldiers and ward off tanks. Packed together, they gave off a blast of heat, as though every one of them was a blazing torch.

This was a key moment in my life. I had always assumed that light carries farther than human voices and voices carry farther than body heat. But that night I realized it is not so, for when the people stand as one, their voices carry farther than light and their heat is carried farther still. That, I discovered, is what "the people" means.

领袖
leader

The leader* I have in mind here is one who enjoys a special prerogative. When reviewing the National Day parade from Tiananmen, the Gate of Heavenly Peace, he alone can wave to the marchers as they pass; other members of the ruling elite can only stand at his side and clap their hands. There is just one leader, of course, who fits this description. His name is Mao Zedong. During the Cultural Revolution years Mao would wear a military uniform when he stood on Tiananmen and—maybe because he was happy or maybe just because he was hot—would often take off his cap and wave it at the assembled multitude in the square below.

At the outset of the Cultural Revolution "big-character posters" started to appear. Political screeds rendered in clumsily handwritten characters—and now and again some elegantly written ones, too—these were the first acts of the disenfranchised masses in challenging the power of officialdom. Written on broadsheets as big as decent-sized windows and posted on the walls that ran alongside city streets, shorter versions took the form of two sheets of paper mounted one on top of the other, while longer ones

lingxiu

involved five or six sheets set out in a horizontal row. In the years to follow, these big-character posters would become the largest exhibition of calligraphy China has ever seen: all across the country, in cities and towns, big streets and small, walls were decorated with them. People would gather in the streets and read the posters with undisguised relish, for although they all employed much the same revolutionary rhetoric, they began to criticize officials and their high and mighty ways.

In Mao a politician's grasp of the historical moment was coupled with a poet's whimsy, and it was often through some improvised flourish that he would unveil his program. When the Communist Party Central Committee and the top brass in Beijing tried to clamp down on popular protests, Mao did not use his supreme authority as party chairman to set his colleagues straight. Instead, he employed the very same approach as the masses by writing a big-character poster of his own, entitled "Bombard the Headquarters," protesting that "some leading comrades" had adopted "the reactionary stand of the bourgeoisie . . . encircling and suppressing revolutionaries" and "stifling opinions different from their own." You can imagine people's reaction: what can it mean when the great leader Chairman Mao has gone so far as to write a big-character poster? It can mean only one thing—that Chairman Mao is in the same boat as ordinary people like themselves! No wonder, then, that the great proletarian Cultural Revolution soon engulfed China with the speed of an unquenchable wildfire.

Historically, emperors have always cut the kind of figure and spoken the kind of language expected of an emperor, no matter how exalted or how humble their origins. Mao was the only exception. After he became leader, he often acted quite out of keeping with accepted norms, taking his comrades in the Communist Party leadership completely by surprise. Mao understood very well how to whip the masses into a frenzy, and by appearing on the Gate of Heavenly Peace in the early stages of the Cultural Revolution and greeting fanatical "revolutionary students" and "revolutionary masses" there, he impelled the high tide to ever greater heights.

The Yangtze swim was a fine example of our leader's distinctive style. On July 16, 1966, Mao appeared unexpectedly at a mass swimming event in Wuhan. Cheered on by the ecstatic roars of the spectators lining the banks, with the strains of the revolution's anthem, "The East Is Red," blaring from the loudspeakers, Mao, then seventy-two years old, braved the wind and waves in the company of several thousand other swimmers, who, carried away with delight, shouted "Long Live Chairman Mao" at the top of their voices as the Yangtze swirled around them. The water they gulped down as they shouted must have been quite filthy, but when they returned to shore, they were unanimous in pronouncing it "unbelievably sweet." At the end of his swim Mao clambered onto a boat, hitched up his swimming trunks, and waved majestically to the dense throngs lining the banks. After a brief wave he ducked into the cabin to change. In the newsreel documentary released after the event, the scene of him waving was edited in such a way that Mao appeared to be waving to the people for a good couple of minutes. If you count the propaganda posters that freeze-framed this famous moment and reproduced it endlessly during the Cultural Revolution, then Mao's wave lasted a full ten years.

The next day the *People's Daily* had this to say: "It is the greatest joy of the Chinese people—and of the revolutionary peoples of the entire world—that our revered leader, Chairman Mao, is in such excellent health!" Mao himself wrote about swimming the Yangtze in one of his lyric poems: "Let the wind blow and waves beat / Better far than idly strolling in a courtyard."* With such offhand gestures this leader of ours propelled the Cultural Revolution forward into the madness that would follow.

The film of Mao's swim was shown repeatedly inside China and out, and posters commemorating the event lined the walls of Chinese cities and villages. They showed Mao in his swimsuit, smiling and waving his hand, surrounded by a throng of beaming workers, peasants, soldiers, students, and shop clerks, all striking eager, attentive poses. What other political figure would make a point of waving to his people in a swimsuit? Only Mao could carry this off.

It was a style that, in fact, preceded his becoming China's leader, for we see evidence of it during the War of Resistance Against Japan, when he was living a hardscrabble life in the caves of Yan'an. During an interview with an American reporter Mao groped around in the crotch of his pants, catching lice, as he confidently predicted China's victory over the Japanese.

Once the Cultural Revolution was launched, Mao kept on waving, but the party officials around him stopped clapping. Instead, their right hands would be doing a little wave of their own, because they would be clutching copies of *Quotations from Chairman Mao*. The Little Red Book, as it was called, had given them a chance to wave as well, though they never dared raise their hands as high as Mao or swing them in as wide an arc.

In the Cultural Revolution, even when Mao was not present, the party officials would wave the Little Red Book as a way of greeting the revolutionary masses. Just as today no famous actress would ever appear in public without makeup, the leadership in those days would never show their faces

Mao Tsetung Poems (Peking: Commercial Press, 1962), p. 62.

without the Little Red Book in hand. It was their political makeup kit.

Today the Chinese Communist Party takes the form of a collective leadership, and when the nine members of the Politburo Standing Committee attend a news conference, they wave simultaneously to reporters, their hands at the same height, waving in the same arc. This always makes me think of Mao on Tiananmen, and of how impressive it was that he waved and everyone else clapped. Reflecting on the past in the light of the present, I have a sense that in today's China we no longer have a leader—all we have is a leadership.

Many years after the 1976 death of a genuine leader, ersatz leaders are sprouting up everywhere in China. Since 1990, as beauty contests have swept across the country, competitions to select different kinds of leaders have followed hot on their heels—contests to decide fashion leaders and elegance leaders, leaders in charm and leaders in beauty.

Although there are many varieties of beauty contests, they ultimately are all somewhat confined in scope. For example, there's the Silver-haired Beauty Contest for women over sixty, the Tipsy Beauty Contest for pretty girls who have knocked back a few shots, and the Artificial Beauty Contest for veterans of plastic surgery.

Contests for leaders, on the other hand, are not subject to any particular limitations, and so leaders from every walk of life are emerging thick and fast. Youth leaders, child leaders, future leaders, innovation leaders, real estate leaders, IT leaders, media leaders, commercial leaders, and enterprise leaders—their numbers make one's head spin. With so many leaders on the loose, there are naturally lots of summit meetings to go along with them—summits that make practically as many claims for themselves as does the G8. Leadership contests even extend to geography and technology, so that now we have leaders in natural scenery and leaders among elevators. Such is China in the post-Mao era: even elevators have leaders. When the sun comes up tomorrow, who knows in what corner of the land we'll find a new pack of leaders sprouting up. If we were to hold a contest to choose the word that has lost the most value the fastest during the past thirty years, the winner would surely have to be "leader."

In the Cultural Revolution, however, "leader" was a powerful, sacred word, a synonym for "Chairman Mao"— Mao's exclusive property, one might say. Nobody then would have had the temerity to claim that they were a leader, not even in their dreams. "Sacred and inviolable is the motherland" was a line much favored in those days, and "sacred and inviolable" could equally well have applied to the word "leader"—and to the surname Mao as well.

In the little town where my wife grew up there was a workers' union whose branch chairman was named Mao. "Chairman Mao" was what the locals called him, naturally enough, and it was a name he answered to quite readily. But as a result he became a target in the Cultural Revolution: he had set himself up as a second Chairman Mao, and there was hell to pay. Stung by the charge, he tried strenuously to defend himself, tears streaming down his face. "That's what other people call me," he cried. "It's not what I call myself!" But the revolutionary masses would have none of it. "Other people can call you that if they want," they said, "but you shouldn't have answered them. By acknowledging the title, you were counterrevolutionary."

When I was little, I thought it very unfortunate that I had the surname Yu and wished there had been a Mao on either my father's or my mother's side of the family, not realizing that for ordinary folk like us Mao was a name that projected authority but could be dangerous, too.

Another figure of speech was much in vogue in those days: the Communist Party was "mother of the people." If there's a mother, I thought to myself, then there has to be a father, so who is the people's father? The answer was obvious: Chairman Mao. Logically, the Communist Party was Mao's first lady, but where did that leave Madame Mao, Jiang Qing? Being a junior Red Guard, I knew only of monogamy and the equality of the sexes, not realizing that men in the old society used to have concubines and never imagining that in two or three decades it would be common for men to have mistresses and second wives. Much as I racked my brains, I never found a solution that could reconcile the legitimate claims of both Mao's partners.

Apart from Mao I was aware of four other leaders, all foreign. In my first-grade classroom Mao's portrait hung on the blackboard, and on the wall behind were arrayed the portraits of Marx, Engels, Lenin, and Stalin—the first foreigners I ever saw. For us, Lenin's and Stalin's hairstyles fell within the normal range of men's haircuts, but we didn't know what to make of Marx and Engels, whose hair was long even by women's standards, for women in our town—like Chinese women everywhere then—cropped their hair short below the ear. Hair length was the established yardstick for distinguishing the sexes, and so Marx and Engels left us baffled, especially Marx—his curly hair practically covered his ears, much like the women of our town, whose ears revealed themselves only occasionally beneath their thick heads of hair. Marx's bushy beard, of course, tended to deter us from further speculation about his gender. One of my classmates, however, brushed aside this evidence and went so far as to publicly declare, "Marx was a woman."

For that he almost ended up being branded as a little

counterrevolutionary. He wouldn't have been the first, of course. One girl in second grade had folded a portrait of Mao in such a way that a cross had appeared on his face; somebody informed on her, and we all called her "the little counterrevolutionary." She broke down in tears at the school assembly where her crime was reported, and she blubbered so much when making her confession that we could hardly follow what she was saying.

Afterward our first-grade teacher called our class together and asked us to expose other little counterrevolutionaries who might have burrowed their way into our ranks. Fingers of suspicion were pointed at two young children. The first had a name unknown to us, and it took some time for the teacher to establish that he was the three-year-old son of the informer's neighbor, guilty late one afternoon of a reactionary comment. "The sun went down," he had been heard to say. In those days Mao was commonly compared to a bright red sun, so the sun was not something to be talked of lightly, and at nightfall the most one could say was "It's getting dark." For him to say "The sun went down" was tantamount to saying "Mao Zedong went down."

The second suspect was the classmate who had identified Marx as a woman. White as a sheet, he completely fell to pieces under the teacher's questioning. Tears streamed from his eyes and snivel dripped from his nose when he was asked whether he had indeed uttered such a reactionary remark. "I think maybe"—he gave a cough—"I—I did say that."

Our teacher offered him a chance to rephrase his statement: "You think maybe you said it, or you think maybe you didn't say it?"

The panic-stricken boy responded with a welter of sobbing and confusion, one minute saying he thought maybe he'd said it, the next minute saying he thought maybe he hadn't. Right to the end of the denunciation meeting he was still going back and forth between one answer and the other. By sowing doubt in the minds of his listeners, "I think maybe" turned out to be his salvation, for in the end nothing came of it.

For a brief period when I was small, I was under the impression that Chairman Mao was our leader's full name. "Chairman Mao" was on everyone's lips, and one said it unthinkingly, with even more warmth than when one said "Grandpa" or "Daddy." With time, because people were always chanting "Long Live Mao Zedong Thought!" and singing "The east is red, the sun is rising, / China has brought forth a Mao Zedong," I came to understand that Chairman Mao was actually a combination of surname and official rank and that Mao Zedong was his true name. To refer to him in that way in normal conversation, of course, would have been the height of disrespect.

During the Dragon Boat Festival of 2009 the following text message began to circulate:

New China News Agency, May 28: The Chinese Academy of Sciences has successfully cloned Mao Zedong; the clone's physical indicators match those of Mao in his prime. This announcement has elicited a powerful reaction internationally. U.S. President Obama has declared that within three days the United States will repeal the Taiwan Relations Act and withdraw all military forces stationed in Asia. The prime minister of Japan has ordered the demolition of the Yasukuni Shrine, acknowledged that the Senkaku Islands are Chinese territory, and approved reparations for the 1937 invasion of China to the tune of 13 trillion dollars. The European Union has lifted its ban on arms sales to China. Russia's President Medvedev has conceded China's claim to a million square miles in eastern Siberia. Mongolia has signaled to the United Nations that it has always been part of China. Taiwan's President Ma Ying-jeou has promised to abide by all arrangements proposed by the mainland regarding reunification and has applied to be a scholar at the National Archives. North Korean leader Kim Jong-il has sent instructions to his representative at the Six Party Talks to handle things according to Chairman Mao's directives. There has been a rapid turnaround in domestic affairs: in just twenty-four hours officials from the county level and up have returned their ill-gotten gains, to the tune of 980 trillion yuan;* privately run businesses have converted to public ownership; 25 million sex hostesses have become honest women overnight; the stock market has soared; house prices have declined by 60 percent; the Chinese people once more are singing the anthem of the age: "The east is red, the sun is rising, / China has brought forth another Mao Zedong."

By changing "China has brought forth a Mao Zedong" to "China has brought forth another Mao Zedong," popular humor has resurrected this long-dead leader, imagining how his comeback would awe the world, strike fear into the hearts of China's corrupt bureaucrats, and solve at one fell swoop the historical problems, diplomatic issues, and domestic crises that plague China today. What, I wonder, are the wider implications of this overheated fantasy? A sign of discontent with contemporary realities? Evidence of neo-nationalist fervor? Or is it just a joke, a wry reflection on the time and place in which we live? All of these, perhaps, and probably other things as well.

In the thirty-odd years since Mao's death China has fashioned an astonishing economic miracle, but the price it has paid is even more astounding. When I left South Africa at the end of a visit during the 2010 World Cup, the duty-free shop at Johannesburg's airport was selling vuvuzelas—Chinese-made plastic horns—for the equiva-

*In the spring of 2011, the exchange rate of the Chinese yuan stood at about 6.5 yuan to the U.S. dollar.

lent of 100 yuan each, but on my return home I learned that the export price was only 2.6 yuan apiece. One company in Zhejiang manufactured 20 million vuvuzelas but ended up making a profit of only about 100,000 yuan. This example gives a sense of China's lopsided development: year after year chemical plants will dump industrial waste into our rivers, and although a single plant might succeed in generating a thirty-million-yuan boost to China's GDP, to clean up the rivers it has ruined will cost ten times that amount. An authority I respect has put it this way: China's model of growth is to spend 100 yuan to gain 10 yuan in increased GDP. Environmental degradation, moral collapse, the polarization of rich and poor, pervasive corruption—all these things are constantly exacerbating the contradictions in Chinese society. More and more we hear of mass protests in which hundreds or even thousands of people will burst into a government compound, smashing up cars and setting fire to buildings.

Many Chinese have begun to pine for the era of Mao Zedong, but I think the majority of them don't really want to go back in time and probably just feel nostalgic. Although life in the Mao era was impoverished and restrictive, there was no widespread, cruel competition to survive, just empty class struggle, for actually there were no classes to speak of in those days and so struggle mostly took the form of sloganeering and not much else. People then were on an equal level, all alike in their frugal lifestyles; as long as you didn't stick your neck out, you could get through life quite uneventfully.

China today is a completely different story. So intense is the competition and so unbearable the pressure that, for many Chinese, survival is like war itself. In this social environment the strong prey on the weak, people enrich themselves through brute force and deception, and the meek and humble suffer while the bold and unscrupulous flourish.

Changes in moral outlook and the reallocation of wealth have created a two-tiered society, and this in turn generates social tensions. So in China today there have emerged real classes and real class conflict.

After Mao, Deng Xiaoping drew on his own personal prestige to implement reforms and pursue an open-door policy, but in his final years he came to reflect on the paradox that even more problems had emerged after development than existed before it. Perhaps this is precisely why Mao keeps being brought back to life. Not long ago a public opinion poll asked people to anticipate their reaction if Mao were to wake up today. Ten percent thought it would be a bad thing, 5 percent thought it would have no impact on China or the world, and 85 percent thought it would be a good thing. I am unclear about the sample's demographics, but since the respondents were all Internet users, I suspect they were mostly young people. Chinese youth today know very little about Mao Zedong, so their embracing the idea of Mao's resurrection tells us something about the mood of the age. Gripped by the zeitgeist, people of diverse backgrounds and disparate opinions find a common channel for their discontent and—half in earnest, half in jest—act out a ritual of restoring the dead to life.

In an online discussion of this scenario, someone cracked the following joke:

> Mao rises from his glass coffin and walks out onto the steps of his mausoleum as morning sunshine bathes Tiananmen Square. A bunch of tourists dash to his side. "Gu Yue," they cry. "Give us your autograph, will you?"

Gu Yue, you see, is an actor famous for playing Mao.

When I was in primary school, I firmly believed China to be the greatest country in the world. I had two reasons for thinking that way. The first was that we had a great leader in Chairman Mao, whereas the four foreign leaders on my classroom wall—Marx, Engels, Lenin, and Stalin—had all died, so other countries did not have any great leaders. The second reason was that China had the biggest population, and Chairman Mao had said the more the people, the greater their strength.

When Chairman Mao's Three-World Theory appeared in the newspapers and on the radio, I was shaken to the core. It had never occurred to me that the American imperialists and the Soviet revisionists would be the first world, Japan and European countries the second, and our great nation of China would be lumped together in the third world with the little countries of Asia, Africa, and Latin America.

But how could an ignorant little boy like me appreciate Mao Zedong's grand vision? After the victory of the Chinese revolution Mao was never content with what he had gained, never satisfied with just being leader of his own nation. He wanted to become the leader of all exploited and oppressed peoples. "Wherever there are contradictions, there will be oppression," he said loftily, "and wherever there is oppression, there will be resistance." As his attention shifted to a global agenda, he developed an urge to liberate all the proletarians of the world—and acted on this impulse by exporting revolution.

Many years have passed since then. Putting aside for the moment the question of Mao's impact, positive and negative, on China, one thing is clear: Mao Zedong Thought has not perished just because his life came to an end. On the contrary, his influence beyond our borders is undiminished. For many people in many parts of the world, I have found, what Mao did in China is not so important—what matters is that his ideas retain their vitality and, like seeds planted in receptive soil, "strike root, flower, and bear fruit."

A couple of years ago Austrians raised aloft huge portraits of Marx, Engels, Lenin, Stalin, and Mao at a big May Day parade in Vienna. Similar sights can be observed in other European cities, making one wonder whether the Mao revival is not just a mentality peculiar to China but more of a global phenomenon. If so, what does this mean? The simplest answer might be this: when the world is ailing, revolutionary impulses are stirred, just as when the body is ailing, inflammation ensues.

In November 2008 I visited Nepal as a member of a writers' delegation. The Unified Communist Party of Nepal (Maoist) had claimed victory in the spring legislative elections and its leader, Prachanda, had recently become prime minister in the new government. During our visit we traveled through a United Nations peacekeepers' base to visit a camp of the Nepalese Communist (Maoist) Liberation Army. Its facilities were primitive, and the troops lacked guns and ammunition, but this unarmed army maintained strict discipline. A memorable sight greeted us as we entered one of their huts: just as in my primary school classroom, on the wall were portraits of Marx, Engels, Lenin, Stalin, and Mao—along with Prachanda, of course. The increase of faces from five to six seemed simply to demonstrate that revolution shows no signs of abating. That evening we had a get-together with the army members, and after several rounds of toasts we all stood up and sang "Long March," a Cultural Revolution anthem inspired by one of Mao's poems. We sang in Chinese, and the soldiers sang in Nepali. I doubt we were thinking about the same things, but when we sang the anthem in our two languages, it seemed as though we were all singing in one.

During the Cultural Revolution it wasn't just Mao's poems that were put to music; his quotations were, too. They were sung by adults and children, by scholars and illiterates, by politically correct masses and by landlords, rich peasants, counterrevolutionaries, bad elements, and rightists. Seen in that light, Mao must be rated the most influential author in Chinese history.

Mao's poems and quotations were everywhere, then. From city to village, on brick walls and mud walls, interior walls and outside walls, every space was covered with them, along with the gleaming image of Mao Zedong. On the bowls out of which we ate our rice was printed Mao's maxim "Revolution is not a dinner party," and the mugs out of which we drank our water were embellished with lines from Mao's lyric on swimming in the Yangtze: "I have just drunk the waters of Changsha / And now I come to eat the fish of Wuchang." In our daily encounters with Mao's pronouncements, the most ordinary things would take on weighty meaning: as we got ready for bed, on our pillowcases we would read "Never forget class struggle" and, on our sheets, "Advance bravely through wind and waves." Mao's image was stenciled inside toilets, and sayings of his decorated our spittoons. Now I realize that these were two places where Mao clearly did not belong, but in those days, strange as it seems, this point escaped us. "Chairman Mao is at our side," people used to say, and I believed that, too. I was certain he'd be happy if I did something good and disappointed if I did something bad.

The most blissful moments in my childhood were when I dreamed of Mao. This happened three times. In one of the dreams he came up to me, ruffled my hair affectionately, and favored me with a few words. What elation I felt! I went off, pleased as punch, to tell my little companions about my audience with Chairman Mao. To my dismay, not one of them believed me. "How could you possibly have seen Chairman Mao?" they snorted. "How could he possibly have come to talk to you?" They were right, of course. "Chairman Mao is at our side" was just one of those flights of fancy typical of the Cultural Revolution, conjured into being by the very ubiquity of those golden busts of Mao and those quotations in bold red script. The Mao Zedong of down-to-earth reality was hazy and distant; he existed only in symbolic terms. Mao was so remote that, as my childhood playmates said, there was no chance of our ever meeting him, not even in a dream.

During the Cultural Revolution one of the locals returned from a trip to Beijing claiming he had shaken hands with Mao Zedong. Crying tears of joy, he told everyone how warmly the chairman had greeted him—even asking him his name! Chairman Mao had shaken his hand for a good four seconds before somebody else had displaced him. "It would have been five if not for that other guy!" he lamented.

This man naturally became a hero in our town, and I would often see him striding proudly down the street with a faded green military satchel on his back. Because his right hand had held Mao's hand, he did not wash it once in the year that followed, and somehow it looked bigger than his left hand—as well as black and grimy as a bear's paw. Everyone in our town who knew him would make a point of shaking this bear paw of his. "I shook the hand that Chairman Mao has shaken," they would tell their neighbors ecstatically.

When I grew up and exchanged stories about the Cultural Revolution with friends from other parts of China, I would often mention this man, only to find they knew of similar individuals in their home districts—sometimes more than one. So I began to suspect that our small-town hero just made it all up, for surely it wasn't so easy to shake Mao's hand. I think our man was probably squeezed into a thick scrum of people packed together on Tiananmen Square during one of the chairman's grand inspections, watching Mao in the far, far distance as he stood on the Gate of Heavenly Peace and waved his hand in greeting. He dimly saw Mao's hand and imagined himself shaking it—and when everyone in our town became convinced this had happened, he became convinced of it, too.

In those days Mao Zedong's portrait shimmered like the sun on the Gate of Heavenly Peace, its dimensions quite out of proportion to the size of the gate. Almost every day I would see his awe-inspiring image on one wall or another of our little town, and almost every day we would sing a song that went:

I love Beijing's Tiananmen
Splendid under morning sun.
Our Great Leader Chairman Mao
Leads us forward, on and on.

I used to have a photograph of myself when I was fifteen, standing in the middle of Tiananmen Square with Mao's huge portrait visible in the background. It was taken not in Beijing but in the photography studio of our town a thousand miles away. The room in which I was standing cannot have been more than twenty feet wide, and the square was just a theatrical backdrop painted on the wall. When you looked at the photo, you might almost have believed I was really standing in Tiananmen Square—except for the complete absence of people in the acres of space behind me.

This photograph crystallized the dreams of my childhood years—and, indeed, the dreams of most Chinese children who lived in other places than Beijing. Almost all studios then were equipped with this same tableau of Tiananmen, designed to satisfy our vicarious desires, for to us in the provinces the Gate of Heavenly Peace might just as well have been Mao Zedong's front door. Hence that picture—now lost, I regret to say—of me standing at the entrance to Mao's imagined home.

My yearning for the Gate of Heavenly Peace was simply an extension of my eagerness to see Mao. During the

Cultural Revolution a documentary featuring Mao and Tiananmen would be filmed every year on National Day, October 1. Often by the time the newsreel made it to our little town it would be well into winter. I would head off down the street in my lumpy padded jacket as a bitter night wind blew in my face, then sit down in the unheated cinema and watch the grainy images of autumnal Tiananmen, where Mao was waving to the marchers.

What left the deepest impression on me from the National Day newsreels was the pyrotechnics display that took place after nightfall, when Mao and his colleagues sat down at a table so groaning with fruits and pastries it made my mouth drool. Fireworks illuminated the square as brightly as day: for me as a boy this was the most exhilarating scene of all. In our town major holidays were celebrated by letting off a few firecrackers at most, and to see so many fireworks explode in the sky for so many minutes, even if it was only on the screen, was enough to leave me speechless with wonder.

In later documentaries Prince Sihanouk, then recently deposed as ruler of Cambodia, appeared, smiling infectiously at Mao's side, along with the prince's onetime prime minister, Penn Nouth, who would cock his head and nod obsequiously as they spoke. Already well into my fantasy-rich adolescence by this time, I became quite besotted with Sihanouk and Penn Nouth's lovely young wives; every time they showed up in National Day footage, I thought to myself, "Now things are getting interesting!" The daytime parade and the after-dark fireworks had lost their appeal; Sihanouk and Penn Nouth had become the two men I envied most in the world, particularly the latter—clearly over the hill, I thought, and not even capable of holding his head up straight, but still with a lissome beauty at his beck and call.

I owe my most lasting memories of Mao to the ceiling of my house. We would have seen right up to the roof tiles if every year my father hadn't pasted a new layer of newspapers over them to prevent dust, to make our ceiling more presentable, and to give us a feeling of insulation. My childhood was spent under this canopy of newsprint: I could read all the headlines from my bed, although the text itself was impossible to make out. When Mao first appeared on my ceiling, he had Liu Shaoqi standing next to him, but before long Liu had disappeared, to be replaced by Lin Biao, who soon performed a vanishing trick as well; finally Mao was joined by a young Cultural Revolution militant named Wang Hongwen.* In the National Day photo spread, the people by Mao's side kept changing; Mao alone remained constant from one year to the next. As the newspapers were refreshed annually, I was witness to Mao's physical decline; his increasing senility on my bedroom ceiling was brought to an abrupt halt when the paper stopped printing a photograph of Mao on National Day and replaced it with the generic image displayed everywhere in the country.

One morning in September 1976, when I was in my second year of high school, we all stood to attention as usual before the start of class and barked in chorus to the official image of Mao above the blackboard: "We wish Great Leader Chairman Mao eternal long life!" Then we sat down and began to read aloud a paragraph in our textbook. In those days all essays used the exact same phrases to describe Mao: "Glowing with health, radiating vigor." This language had been introduced in the textbook during my first year of elementary school, and it appeared without the slightest alteration in the one we used ten years later. No sooner had we finished reciting these lines than the school's PA

*Liu Shaoqi, appointed China's head of state in 1959, was denounced early in the Cultural Revolution as the Communist Party's "biggest capitalist roader" and in 1968 was dismissed from all his positions. Lin Biao became Mao's second-in-command in 1969 but perished in a plane crash in 1971 after what was said to be an unsuccessful coup attempt. Wang Hongwen rose rapidly through party ranks and in 1973 was elevated to third place in the hierarchy.

system interrupted us with a sudden blare. It instructed all staff and students to assemble at once in the auditorium; an important broadcast would follow at 9 a.m.

We picked up our chairs, all one thousand of us, and shuffled into the auditorium, where we sat down and waited. Half an hour passed, and at nine o'clock funereal music sounded. I instantly had a grim sense of foreboding. Two senior leaders of the Communist Party had died that year—first Zhou Enlai, then Zhu De, just a few days before—so we knew what was coming.

The long dirge came to an end, and a grief-stricken voice began to intone a slow litany of titles: "The Central Committee of the Chinese Communist Party, the Military Commission of the Chinese Communist Party, the State Council of the People's Republic of China, the National People's Congress, the National Political Consultative Conference. . . ."

It seemed to take forever to get to the obituary notice issued by these supreme organs of power. Another ponderous, doleful recitation began: "Great Leader, Great Teacher, Great Commander, Great Helmsman. . . ." Finally, after this long string of epithets, came the real substance: Chairman Mao Zedong had passed away after a long illness. Even before the final words, "aged eighty-two," the auditorium was already seething with moans and wails.

Our leader was dead. My eyes too filled with tears, and I wept like the thousand others. I heard heartrending screeches and earthshaking howls, people gasped for breath and choked in anguish—and then my mind began to wander. Grief no longer held me in its sway; my thoughts started moving in another direction entirely. If it had been just a few people weeping, I would certainly have felt sad, but a thousand people all weeping at the same time simply struck me as funny. I had never in my life heard such a cacophony. Even if every living variety of beast were to send a delegate to our auditorium and they were all to bellow in unison, I thought to myself, they surely could not make a stranger chorus than the din of a thousand people crying their heads off.

This untimely fancy might have been the death of me. I couldn't help but smile, and then I had to fight back the laugh that was pushing its way out. If anybody were to see me laughing, I would be labeled a counterrevolutionary on the spot and life would not be worth living. Hard as I tried to bottle up my laughter, it insisted on spilling forth, and knowing I couldn't stifle it any longer, I desperately threw myself forward, hugging the back of the chair in front of me, and buried my head in my folded arms. Amid the weeping of a thousand people I was in the throes of uncontainable mirth, my shoulders heaving, and the more I tried to stop myself from laughing, the more the laughs kept coming.

My classmates, through a curtain of tears, saw me sprawled over a chair, racked by agonizing spasms of grief. They were deeply moved by my devotion to our fallen leader, and later they would say, "Yu Hua was more upset than anyone—you should have seen the way he was crying."

阅读

reading

S ince I grew up in a time and a place where there were no books, it's hard to say just how I began to read. But sorting through my memories, I find my earliest reading* experiences fall into four sequences.

T he first dates back to the summer following my graduation from elementary school, in 1973. By then we were into the seventh year of the Cultural Revolution, and the bloody street battles and savage house lootings were now well behind us. Cruelties perpetrated in the name of the revolution seemed to have worn themselves out, leaving life in our small town in a quiescent state, stifled and repressed. People had become more timid and circumspect than before, and although the newspapers and radio broadcasts carried on promoting class struggle day after day, it seemed ages since I had seen a class enemy.

At this point the town library, which had been mothballed for so long, finally reopened. My father managed to wangle a reader's card for my brother and me, to give us something to do during the tedious vacation. Thus began my reading

*yuedu

36

of fiction. In China then, practically all literary works were labeled "poisonous weeds." Works by foreign authors such as Shakespeare, Tolstoy, and Balzac were poisonous weeds; works by Chinese authors like Ba Jin, Lao She, and Shen Congwen were poisonous weeds; and with the falling-out between Mao and Khrushchev, revolutionary literature of the Soviet era had become poisonous weeds, too. Since the bulk of the library's holdings had perished in all the Red Guard book burning, there was very little left to read. The fiction shelf featured only twenty-odd titles, all so-called socialist revolutionary literature of the homegrown variety. I read all these books in turn: *Bright Sunny Skies, The Golden Road, Ox-field Strand, Battle Song of Hongnan, New Bridge, Storm over Mine Shaft Hill, Spring Comes to the Land of Flying Snow, Glittering Red Star. . . .* My favorites were *Glittering Red Star* and *Storm over Mine Shaft Hill,* for the simple reason that their protagonists were children.

This kind of reading has left no traces on my life, for in these books I encountered neither emotions nor characters nor even stories. All I found was grindingly dull accounts of class struggle. This did not stop me from reading each book through to the end, because my life at the time was even more grindingly dull. "A starving man isn't picky," we say in Chinese, and that sums up my reading in those days. So long as it was a novel, so long as there were still some pages to go, I would keep on reading.

A few years ago two retired professors of Chinese in Berlin told me about their experience during the Great Famine of 1959–62. They were studying at Peking University at the time, and the husband had to return home early to deal with a family emergency. Two months later he received a letter from his wife. "Things are awful here," it said. "The students have eaten all the leaves off the trees." Just as the famished students stripped the campus trees bare, so I devoured every one of those grim, unappetizing novels on the library shelf.

The librarian was a middle-aged woman very dedicated to her profession. Every time my brother, Hua Xu, and I returned a book, she would inspect it meticulously and not let us borrow another until she had satisfied herself that the returned volume had suffered no damage at our hands. Once she noticed an ink spot on the cover of the book we were returning and held us responsible. No, we had nothing to do with that, we told her—the ink spot had been there all the time. She stuck to her guns, insisting she always checked every book and there was no way she would have missed such a glaring stain. We began to argue, an activity known at the time as "civil struggle." Hua Xu was a Red Guard, and he saw civil struggle as a wimpy sort of activity; "martial struggle" was more the Red Guard style. So he picked up the book and threw it in her face, then gave her a clip across the ear for good measure.

After that we all went to the local police station, where the librarian sat in a chair for a long time, drenched in tears, while Hua Xu strolled back and forth in a show of calm indifference. The station chief did his best to console the woman, at the same time cursing out my brother and telling him to sit down and behave. So Hua Xu sat down and crossed his legs nonchalantly. The station chief was a friend of my father's, and I had once asked his advice about what to do in a fight. He had sized me up briefly—I was a puny little boy—and then given me the following tip: nip in before your adversary is ready and kick him in the balls. "What if it's a girl?" I asked.

"Boys don't fight with girls," he told me sternly.

My brother's demonstration of Red Guard fighting prowess lost us our reader's card. But I found this no cause for regret, because by then I had read all the novels in the library. The problem was that the summer vacation was far from over and my appetite for reading was sharper than ever.

At home all we had was the dozen or so medical books my parents had acquired in the course of their professional training, plus the four-volume set of *Selected Works of Mao Zedong* and *Quotations from Chairman Mao*—the Little Red Book, a compilation of sayings culled from *Selected Works*. I fingered these books listlessly, waiting for some chemistry to develop, but even after much turning of pages I found I had not the slightest inclination to read them.

So I had no choice but to leave the house and, like a man with a rumbling stomach on a search for food, I went off on a hunt for books. Dressed in a pair of shorts and a tank top, with flip-flops on my feet, I roamed the sunbaked streets and greeted every boy I knew with the call, "Hey, got any books at home?"

The other boys, all dressed exactly like me, gave a start when they heard my inquiry, for it was most likely the first time they had ever been asked such a question. They would nod their heads: "Yeah, we do." But when I ran to their houses, full of excitement, all I saw was that familiar four-volume edition of *Selected Works of Mao Zedong*—always a new, unopened set. This taught me a lesson, and so the next time one of my respondents told me he had books at home I stuck out four fingers. "Four books, you mean?" When he nodded, my hand would drop to my side. "New books, right?" I would ask. When he nodded once more, I could not conceal my disappointment. "Oh, not *Selected Works* again!"

Later I changed my opening question. "Got old books?" I would ask.

The boys I met shook their heads—with one exception. This boy blinked, then nodded. "I think so," he said.

"Four books?" I asked.

He shook his head. "Just one, I think."

But that could mean the Little Red Book. "Has it got a red cover?"

He thought for a moment. "Gray, I think."

Now I was getting somewhere. His threefold iteration of "I think" raised my confidence enormously. I clapped my sweaty hand on his sweaty shoulder and treated him to such an endless stream of compliments that he was practically purring with pleasure by the time we got to his house. There he bustled about, moving a stool in front of the wardrobe, then groping around on top of the wardrobe until he finally got his hand on a small book caked with dust, which he presented to me. I immediately felt uneasy, for it was a pocketbook much the same size as *Quotations from Chairman Mao*. When I scraped away the thick layer of dust that coated the jacket, my heart sank at the sight of a red plastic cover—it was the Little Red Book.

All my efforts outside having proved fruitless, I had no choice but to try to tap latent potential at home—to "increase internal demand to stimulate growth," to borrow today's catchphrase. I had a cursory glance through the medical books and then put them right back on the shelf, completely failing to notice the wonders concealed inside their covers and so postponing by two years my discovery of their secrets. After that, all that was left was a brand-new set of *Selected Works of Mao Zedong* and a dog-eared copy of the Little Red Book. That was the situation typical of every household then: *Selected Works* was simply political ornamentation, and it was the Little Red Book that was taken up for study on a daily basis.

I passed over the Little Red Book and opted for *Selected Works* instead. This time I began to read it carefully and in so doing found something I had missed before, which opened up a whole new world. From then on *Selected Works* was seldom out of my hands.

In summertime then everyone ate outdoors. First we would splash a few basins of cold water on the ground, in part to cool things off, in part to keep the dust in place, and then we would bring out a table and stools. Once dinner was served, we children would walk back and forth with our rice bowls in our hands, inspecting the dishes on other tables as we ate up the food in our own bowls. I was always quick to finish my meal; then, after putting down bowl and chopsticks, I would pick up *Selected Works* and read it avidly by the light of the setting sun.

The neighbors all sighed in wonder, impressed that at such a tender age I was already so assiduous in my study of Mao Zedong Thought. My parents brimmed with pride on hearing so much praise. Privately they began in hushed voices to discuss my future, lamenting that the Cultural Revolution had restricted my educational opportunities, for otherwise their younger son would surely be well on his way to becoming a university professor.

In reality Mao Zedong Thought had completely failed to engage me. What I liked to read in *Selected Works* was simply the footnotes, explanatory summaries of historical events and biographical details about historical figures, which proved to be much more interesting than the novels in our local library. Although there was no emotion to be found in the footnotes, they did have stories, and they did have characters.

The second phase of my early reading dates to my high school years, when I began to read poisonous weeds. Some books had somehow managed to escape the bonfires—spirited away, perhaps, by true literature lovers—and these fortunate survivors began surreptitiously to circulate among us. Every one of these books must have passed through the hands of a thousand people or more before they reached me, and so they were in a terrible state of disrepair, with easily a dozen or more pages missing from the beginning and the same number missing at the end. So I knew neither the books' titles nor their authors, neither how the stories began nor how they ended.

To not know how a story began was not such a hardship, but to not know how it ended was a painful deprivation. Every time I read one of these headless, tailless novels I was like an ant on a hot wok, running around everywhere in search of someone who could tell me the ending. But everybody was in the same boat, for the versions other people had read were also missing pages at the beginning and end, and though sometimes I met people who had read a few more pages than I had and could brief me on developments in that portion of the book, they still did not know the final denouement. Such was our experience of reading: our books were constantly losing pages as they passed through the hands of several—or several dozen—readers. It left me disconsolate, mentally cursing those earlier readers who had been able to finish the book but never bothered to stick the pages that had fallen out back in.

How these stories without resolutions made me suffer! Nobody could help me, so I began to think up endings for myself. "The Internationale" puts it well:

> No one will grant us deliverance
> Neither god nor emperor
> To create happiness for man
> We depend on our own labor.

Every night when I went to bed and turned off the light, my eyes would blink as I entered the world of imagination, creating endings to those stories that stirred me so deeply tears would run down my face. It was, I realize now, good training for things to come, and I owe a debt to those truncated novels for sparking creative tendencies in me.

The first foreign novel I ever read was another headless, tailless thing, without author or title, beginning or end. In it for the first time I encountered sexual descriptions; they made me anxious and fearful. When I reached one of these passages, I would raise my head in alarm and glance all around. Only when I was sure nobody was watching would I continue reading, my heart in my mouth.

With the end of the Cultural Revolution, literature staged a comeback, and bookstores were packed with new editions of literary works. I must have bought countless Western novels then, and one night I picked out Maupassant's *Une Vie* for bedtime reading. Well into the story I suddenly shouted, "So this is the one!" It was the same book that, years earlier in headless, tailless form, had me shaking like a leaf.

Of the poisonous weeds I was exposed to as a boy only one appeared to be fully intact, and that was Dumas' *La dame aux camélias.* I was in the second year of high school by then, and the Cultural Revolution was on its last legs. *La dame aux camélias* came to us in manuscript form. Later, when I got to read a printed edition, I realized that the manuscript was actually an abridged version.

At that point Great Leader Mao Zedong had just died and his chosen successor, Wise Leader Hua Guofeng, was enjoying his short spell in the limelight, before the reemergence of Deng Xiaoping. I remember a classmate calling me over and telling me in a low voice that he had borrowed a gem of a book. He glanced around nervously. "It's a love story," he confided. When I heard that, my heart pounded. We burst into a trot and ran all the way to his house. As we gasped for breath my friend pulled from his satchel a manuscript wrapped in glossy white art paper. When I turned the paper over, I gave a start, for *La dame aux camélias* turned out to be wrapped in an official portrait of Wise Leader Hua Guofeng. "You counterrevolutionary, you!" I cried.

He was just as startled as I was, for he hadn't noticed

the wrapping; he said it wasn't he but another counter-revolutionary who was responsible, the one who'd lent him the book. Then we conferred about how to deal with the now crumpled portrait of Hua Guofeng. "Let's toss it in the river," he said.

"Better not," I said. "Safer to burn it." So we disposed of the picture and then turned our attention to the manuscript. It was written in neat characters inside a notebook with a brown paper cover. My friend said he had it for one day only; it had to be returned the next morning. We sat with our heads together—an exciting way to read—and before we were a third of the way through, we were already sighing in wonder. "I had no idea there was such a great novel in the world!" we agreed. But this made us worry about losing it—we wanted to keep it for ourselves. Seeing that the book was not so very long, we decided to stop reading and begin copying, so that we could finish the transcription before the deadline ran out.

My classmate found a notebook his father had never used, and we took turns copying the novel. I started things off, and when my wrist began to ache, he at once took over; when he got tired, I took over. In the late afternoon, knowing that my parents would soon be coming home, we needed to pull up stakes and go somewhere safer. After some discussion we decided that a school classroom was the best bet.

High school classes were on the second floor, middle school classes on the first. Although the classroom doors were locked, there were always windows not securely latched, so we walked along outside until we found a room whose window would open. We clambered in and continued our copying in this unfamiliar room; when it got dark, we turned on the fluorescent ceiling lights and carried on.

As hunger gnawed at our bellies and our eyes and arms grew weary, we pushed some desks together; while one of us copied, the other lay down on this makeshift bed. We kept going until dawn, one copying, one sleeping, with roles changing more and more frequently. At the start each of us could copy for half an hour or more, but later we needed to take a rest every five minutes or so. He would lie down on the desk, and no sooner had he started snoring than I would get up and give him a shake. "Hey, wake up, it's your turn."

And as soon as I was asleep, he would be shaking me: "Hey, get up."

And so, by constantly denying each other sleep, we finally completed our marathon copying mission. We climbed out through the window and headed down the road, yawning all the way. As we parted my friend glanced at the red glow in the eastern sky and handed me our copy. He was going to return the original manuscript and then go straight home to bed.

I got home before my parents were up, hastily gobbled down the cold rice and cold dishes left over from their dinner, and fell asleep right away. Almost at once, it seemed, I was woken by my father's angry roar: he was demanding to know where I had spent the night. I mumbled an ambiguous answer, then turned over and went back to sleep.

I slept till noon that day, skipping school and staying at home to read our copy of *La dame aux camélias*. When we'd begun the transcription, our handwriting had been quite neat and regular, but our characters had become progressively more slipshod the longer the book went on. My own careless handwriting I could read well enough, but I could make neither head nor tail of my classmate's. Frustrated by all the illegible words, I worked myself into a towering rage. When I could stand it no longer, I slipped the notebook inside my jacket and left home in search of my friend.

I found him on the school basketball court, about to shoot a basket. I bellowed out his name, giving him such a start that he turned and looked at me in astonishment. "Come over here!" I cried. "Get over here right now!"

Bristling at my aggressive tone, he flung the ball on the ground. He marched over with fists clenched, sweaty from his game. "What's up with you?" he yelled.

I took the book out of my jacket, waved it under his nose, then slipped it back under my arm. "I can't make out what you've written, you idiot!"

Now he understood. Mopping his face, he followed me with a chuckle into the copse next to the school. There I had him stand by my side as I pulled out the notebook and picked up the story from where I had left off. At frequent intervals I had to break off from my reading to ask him in exasperation, "What the hell are these characters?"

Thus my reading stuttered along until finally I reached the end of *La dame aux camélias*. Despite all the fits and starts, the story and the characters made my heart ache, and it was with great reluctance that I surrendered the notebook to him, my cheeks wet with tears.

That evening I was already asleep when he arrived outside our house, shouting my name furiously. He had found my cursive hand just as illegible as I had found his. So I got out of bed and accompanied him to a spot beneath a streetlamp where, as the rest of the town slept, he read away, utterly absorbed, while I leaned against the pole, yawning incessantly but always on call, faithfully deciphering scrawl after scrawl of misshapen calligraphy.

The third stage in my early reading career opened with street reading—big-character posters, in other words, a unique spectacle bequeathed to us by the Cultural Revolution. In those days, to tear big-character posters off the walls would have counted as counterrevolutionary activity, so new posters had to be stuck on top of old ones and walls became thicker and thicker, as though our town were swathed in an oversized padded jacket.

I didn't get to read big-character posters in the early

stages of the Cultural Revolution, for I had only just entered elementary school, at the age of seven, and with my limited recognition of Chinese characters I could read only the titles of posters—and those with a certain degree of difficulty. My interest lay in the fierce street battles that were taking place. I watched with stunned fascination as the adults in our town waved clubs and shouted, "Defend to the death Great Leader Chairman Mao," battering each other until they had blood streaming down their faces. This left me mystified. If everyone was out to defend Chairman Mao, I thought, why were they so intent on beating each other up?

I was a timid creature then, watching the battles from a safe distance. When a group of attackers charged, I ran away at once, making sure I was well out of slingshot range. My brother, two years older than me, preferred to observe the hostilities close up and would stand with his arms folded, insouciance personified.

Every day we would hang out in the streets, watching the fights that frequently broke out as appreciatively as if we were watching black-and-white films in the cinema; "watching movies" became, indeed, our term for hanging out in the street. A few years later, when wide-screen films in color appeared in the cinema, our slang was updated accordingly. If one boy asked, "Where are you going?" the boy heading out to the street would say, "Off to watch a wide-screen."

It was in middle school that I became enamored of big-character posters. This must have been around 1975, in the closing stages of the Cultural Revolution, when bloody battles had given way to a glum apathy. Although there was no change to the streets themselves, what was happening in the streets was different. To us street kids, wide-screens were not nearly so much fun to watch as the earlier black-and-whites, when the streets were full of uproar and activity, like animated films from Hollywood. In the final years of the Cultural Revolution the streets were silent and subdued, like modernist European art-house movies. As we grew from street urchins to street youths our lives shifted from one idiom to the other. The rhythm of our lives in the mid-1970s had a lot in common with the protracted, static scenes and the slow pans and long shots of art-house cinema.

If I close my eyes now, I can see myself thirty-odd years ago, a schoolboy walking home in patched clothes, wearing khaki gym shoes bleached white from use, a worn satchel slung carelessly across my back, wandering aimlessly down the street past walls covered with big-character posters.

There, caught in that camera frame, that younger version of me was coming to appreciate the pleasure of reading. Just as enjoyment of an art-house movie requires a certain aesthetic perseverance, life in the latter stages of the Cultural Revolution needed to be carefully savored; only then could one discover the wonders hidden behind an unprepossessing exterior.

By 1975 people had been numbed into indifference by big-character posters and seldom read the new exposés that sprouted up overnight. Now well on their way to losing all relevance, posters were becoming merely wallpaper. People would walk right past them without looking, and I did the same—until one day when I noticed a poster with a cartoon attached. Years after stumbling upon the footnotes to *Selected Works of Mao Zedong,* my reading had finally discovered another new continent.

The cartoon took the form of a crudely drawn bed on which a man and a woman were reclining; gaudy colors had been applied to make the picture stand out more. This unusual illustration made my heart thump with excitement. On propaganda posters I was used to seeing revolutionary masses—men and women alike—sticking out their chests in heroic poses, but for a bed to appear alongside them was a complete novelty. Here, on a big-character poster espousing revolutionary values, this clumsy sketch of a couple on a bed had obvious sexual implications. I was all agog.

It was the first poster I had ever seriously spent time reading. Sandwiched between revolutionary slogans and frequent quotations of Chairman Mao were exquisite little passages that told the story of a pair of fornicators in our small town. Although I failed to find very explicit sexual details, the associations it conjured up in my mind were enough to set my heart racing, like a little boat bobbing about on the sea.

The names of the adulterous couple were written right above the garish cartoon. I related the story—with further embellishment and gratuitous details thrown in—to my best friends, who listened spellbound. After that we set off in high spirits to find out where the couple lived and worked.

It did not take more than a few days to track them down. The man lived in an alley on the west side of town. We had to wait outside his house for quite some time before he came back from work. Having been apprehended in flagrante delicto, the man was in no mood for further humiliation. He greeted us with a dark scowl and quickly scuttled into his house. The woman worked in a department store in a town three or four miles away. My friends and I agreed on a particular Sunday to make the trip, undeterred by the distance involved, and we soon found the store. It cannot have been more than a few hundred square feet in size. Inside stood three female shop assistants, and it was not clear to us which of them was the man's bedmate. We stood in the doorway and debated which of the women was the most attractive, before agreeing in the end that not one of them was a looker. Then we yelled the name I'd seen on the poster. One of the women answered at once, turning to look at us in surprise, and we dashed off, whooping with glee.

Such was the barren aridity of that time: to see in the flesh the people featured in a wall-poster love affair was enough to put us in a good mood for days.

As this example suggests, although big-characters posters at this point were as crammed full as ever with sayings of Chairman Mao, passages from the left-wing writer Lu Xun, and revolutionary catchwords of the day, there had been a gradual change in the topics they addressed. As rivalry between factions festered and conflicts grew personal, gossip, insult, and muckraking were the new weapons of choice. Sexual innuendoes were beginning to show up in the poster exposés, for improper sexual relations were popular material when people indulged in character assassination and abuse. Thus I developed a taste for reading the posters and made a point of stopping on the way home from school to see whether any new posters had appeared and any juicy new revelations had emerged.

This kind of reading entailed a great deal of effort for very meager returns, and often several days of poster perusal would turn up absolutely nothing of interest. At first my classmates joined me, infected by my enthusiasm, but it didn't take them long to write off this activity as way too unprofitable; their two days of eager reading had unearthed only a handful of anemic phrases—not nearly as stirring, they said, as my more colorful, enhanced versions. But they urged me to persist in my search, and every morning on the way to school they would sidle up to me expectantly and ask, "Anything new?"

The most earthshaking moment in my poster-reading career came when I discovered an account of a girl's affair with a married man. It featured by far the most detailed content I had ever encountered, with certain passages citing verbatim the confessions written by the lovers after their capture.

This episode had elements of a concert program, beginning with a prelude, when the man took a basket of dirty clothes outside to a well and began to do his washing. His wife, who worked in another part of the country, could go home only one month a year, so a young neighbor began to help him with his laundry. The first few times she put his underpants to one side for him to wash, but before long she took to washing them along with his other clothes. A flirtatious minuet followed: she started to borrow books from him and discuss her reactions to them, in conversations that sometimes took place in his bedroom. That led in turn to a rhapsody, with the consummation of their affair. Once, twice, a third time—and that third time the trap was sprung.

By this point catching fornicators had become a popular sport, largely replacing the revolutionary passions of a few years before. People suffering from sour grapes transmuted their craving for illicit sex into a desire to catch others in the act. As soon as they sniffed out an improper relationship, they would keep the offending parties under strict surveillance, waiting for the moment to strike, when they would come bursting through the door to catch the naked couple as they frolicked. And so it came time for the hapless pair to perform the *Pathétique* Symphony, Cultural Revolution style.

In this poster, one quote from the girl's confession particularly caught my eye. After her first time, she said, she "couldn't sit down." This expression made me hot all over, and set all kinds of thoughts running through my head. That evening I called my friends together and we sat down on the riverbank, sheltered by a row of willow trees as the moonlight shone down between their swaying fronds. "Do you want to know something?" I asked in a hushed tone. "What happens to a girl after she's done it with a man?"

"What?" they asked, a quaver in their voices.

"She can't sit down," I said mysteriously.

"Why not?" they gasped.

Why not? I didn't have a clue either. But that didn't stop me from telling them with airy condescension, "Once you get married, you'll understand why not."

When I look back on this episode now, I realize that for me the big-character posters functioned primarily as a form of erotica. But strange to say, my readings in erotica reached their climax not in the street but in my own home.

Since my parents were doctors, we lived in a dormitory for hospital staff. It was a two-story building, six rooms up and six rooms down, a common staircase connecting the two floors, just like the two-story classroom buildings in school. Eleven hospital staff were housed in the building, two rooms being occupied by my family—Hua Xu and I downstairs, my parents upstairs. The bookshelf in their room was where they kept their small collection of medical reference works.

Hua Xu and I had the job of taking turns cleaning the room upstairs, and we were under instructions to do a thorough job of dusting the shelf. I tended to give it only the most cursory wipe, never imagining that those dull-looking tomes might conceal startling wonders. Browsing through them the summer I'd finished elementary school, I had seen nothing special. But my brother had.

I was in the second year of middle school by this point, and he was in the second year of high school. There were several days in succession when, with my parents away at work, Hua Xu would sneak upstairs with some of his classmates and some strange cries would come from my parents' room.

Downstairs, hearing all this commotion, I began to suspect something fishy. But when I ran upstairs, I found Hua Xu and his friends chatting happily, as though nothing untoward was happening. Though I looked around carefully, I could see nothing out of the ordinary. As soon as

I was back downstairs, the weird noises started up again. And those sounds continued for a good couple of months as my brother's classmates trooped up there day after day— I think all the boys in his year must have made the trip at one time or another.

This convinced me that my parents' room must hold some awful secret. One day, when it was my turn to do the housecleaning, I inspected every corner of the room as minutely as a detective, but my search drew a blank. Then I transferred my attention to the bookshelf, suspecting something had perhaps been slipped inside one of the books. I took each book down and turned its pages one by one. As I began to work my way through *Human Anatomy* the wonder suddenly came into view: a color plate illustrating the female genitalia. If I had been struck by a bolt of lightning, I could not have been more transfixed. I hungrily studied every detail of the photograph, as well as the entire written commentary.

I have no idea whether I too gave a shout of astonishment on my first glimpse of the color plate, for I was too stunned to be capable of noting my reaction. What I do know is that after all those acts of pilgrimage by Hua Xu's classmates, it was now *my* classmates' turn to troop upstairs, their turn to make those strange, involuntary cries that came from somewhere deep inside.

The final reading cycle began in 1977. Now that the Cultural Revolution was over, previously banned books could be published once again. When the works of Tolstoy, Balzac, and Dickens arrived in the local bookstore for the first time, this caused as much sensation as if today a pop star were sighted in some celebrity-deprived suburb: everyone ran to spread the word and craned their necks to see. Given the limited number of volumes in the first consignment shipped to our town, the bookstore posted an announcement that customers would have to line up for a book coupon. Each person was entitled to only one coupon, and each coupon entitled one to purchase only two books.

I remember vividly the scene outside the bookstore that day. Before daybreak there must already have been a good two hundred people in a line outside the bookstore. To be sure of getting a coupon, some had arrived the night before, plunking their stools down outside the door, where they sat in a neat rank and passed the night in conversation. Those who arrived at dawn that morning soon realized they were very late. They remained hopeful nonetheless and joined the long queue.

I was one of these Johnny-come-latelys. When I dashed to the bookstore that morning, I ran the whole way with my right hand in my pocket, clutching tightly a five-yuan note—a princely sum for me at the time—and because only my left arm was swinging freely, I ran with an odd leftward lurch. I thought I would be among the first, only to find that there were at least three hundred people ahead of me. Behind me more continued to arrive, and I could hear them muttering with dismay, "Can you believe this? Up so early and we end up late!"

As the sun rose our assembly was divided into two camps: those who had not slept and those who had. People in the first camp, having endured a night on their stools, felt that their coupons were in the bag, and so for them the issue was: which two books to buy? People in the second camp had run to the bookstore after a good night's sleep, and their question was: how many coupons would be issued? Rumors flew. The stool-sitters at the front predicted there would be a hundred coupons at the most. This notion was roundly rejected by the people standing in line, some of whom thought two hundred coupons a more likely figure, although those behind disagreed—there should be more than that, they said. Coupon estimates continued to rise until someone forecast a total of five hundred. We unanimously ruled this out. There were fewer than four hundred people in line, so if they issued five hundred coupons, then all the trouble we had gone to in queuing up would seem ridiculous.

At seven o'clock the door to the New China Bookstore slowly opened. An exalted, almost mystical sensation surged through me at that moment. Although it was just a shabby old door creaking open on dirty hinges, I could almost see a splendid curtain being drawn aside on a stage, and the bookstore clerk who emerged appeared in my eyes to have the poise of a theater impresario. This transcendent feeling, alas, did not last long. "Fifty coupons only!" the man shouted. "The rest of you can just go home."

Those of us standing in line felt a chill pass through us from head to toe, as though a bucket of cold water had been dumped on our heads in full winter. Some drifted away, disconsolate; some grumbled and moaned; some cursed for all they were worth. I stood rooted to the spot, my right hand still clutching the five yuan, and watched, bereft, as the people at the front filed cheerfully into the store to collect their coupons. For them, the fewer the coupons, the greater the value of their sleepless vigil.

Many of us remained huddled outside the bookstore and watched as people came out, proudly brandishing their purchases. We would gather around somebody we knew and enviously reach out a hand to touch their reprints of *Anna Karenina*, *Le Père Goriot*, and *David Copperfield*. Having lived so long in a reading famine, we found it a matchless pleasure just to feast our eyes on the new covers of these classics. Some generously held the books up to our noses and let us sniff their subtle, inky smell. For me that odor was a heady scent.

Those immediately behind No. 50 were anguish personified. They let loose an endless stream of foul language, and it was hard to tell whether they were cursing themselves

or cursing something else. My neighbors and I in the last
third of the queue felt only a pang of disappointment,
whereas those who had only just missed out on a coupon
were like people who see the duck they have cooked flap
its wings and fly away. Particularly No. 51: just as he was
putting his foot inside the door he was told the coupons
were all gone. He stood there for a moment, then shuffled
off to one side, head down, clutching his stool to his chest,
watching blankly as others marched out with their books
and we gathered around to touch and sniff them. He was so
strangely silent that I turned my head several times to look
at him; it seemed to me he was watching us with a look of
total nonrecognition.

Later I heard some gossip about this No. 51. He had
played cards with three buddies until late the previous
night, then come to the bookstore with his stool. In the
days that followed he would greet his friends with a rueful
refrain: "If we'd stopped just one round sooner, I wouldn't
have been No. 51." And so for a little while No. 51 became
a catchphrase in our town: if someone said, "I'm No. 51
today," what he meant was "I've had such rotten luck."

Now, thirty years later, we have moved from an age without books to an age when there is an excess of them—in
China today, more than two hundred thousand books are
published each year. In the past there were no books to buy,
whereas now there are so many that we don't know which
ones to buy. Once Internet outlets began to sell books at a
discount, traditional bookstores soon followed suit. Books
are now sold in supermarkets and newspaper kiosks, and
pirated books are peddled by traveling salesmen by the side
of the road. Once we saw pirated books only in Chinese, but
now we see them popping up in streets and alleys in English
as well.

The book fair that takes place every year in Beijing's
Ditan Park is as lively as a temple festival. It combines book

sales with lectures on classical literature, demonstrations of folk arts, photography exhibitions, free film showings, and cultural performances, along with fashion, dance, and magic. Banks, insurance companies, and asset management firms promote their financial products. Loudspeakers blare music one minute, lost-person bulletins the next. In this cramped and crowded space, writers and scholars attend book signings while quack doctors take pulses and dispense advice, scribbling prescriptions just as rapidly as the authors sign their books.

A few years ago I was involved in just such a book signing. An incessant din drummed in my ears, as though I were in a factory workshop with machines humming and roaring around me. In a row of temporary tents was piled a huge variety of books, and booksellers held microphones to their mouths and hawked their wares much as small vendors in a farmers' market call out the prices of vegetables and fruit, chickens and ducks, fish and meat. What was most memorable for me was to see bundles of books worth several hundred yuan being sold off for a throwaway price, for 10 or 12 yuan. No sooner did one salesman yell, "Bundle of books for 20 yuan," than another would counter with an even more attractive deal: "Rock-bottom prices! Classics for 10 yuan a bundle!"

Even the book vendors found this a bit unbelievable. "What kind of bookselling is this?" they said to themselves. "We might as well be selling wastepaper!"

So their sales pitch would take a different line: "Come and get it! For what it costs to buy wastepaper you can get yourself a bundle of classics!"

I cannot, however, let this story end amid the calls of the auctioneers at the Ditan Book Fair. I want to go back to that scene outside the bookstore in 1977. Although that morning thirty-odd years ago left me empty-handed, I see it now as the point when I began to embark on a true reading of literature. Within a few months new books did arrive on my shelves, and now my reading was no longer subject to the vagaries of Cultural Revolution politics. Instead, it grew abundant and replete, flowing on continuously like the Yangtze's eternal surge. "What have these thirty years of reading given you?" I am sometimes asked. It is no easier to answer that than to articulate one's reaction to a boundless ocean.

I did once sum up my experience in the following way: "Every time I read one of the great books, I feel myself transported to another place, and like a timid child I hug them close and mimic their steps, slowly tracing the long river of time in a journey where warmth and emotion fuse. They carry me off with them, then let me make my own way back, and it's only on my return that I realize they will always be part of me."

One morning several years ago, my wife and I were walking in the old town of Düsseldorf when we stumbled upon the home of Heinrich Heine, a black house in a row of red houses, even older, it seemed, than the old houses around it. It made me think of a faded photograph where you see a grandfather from another era with his sons on either side of him.

That morning took me back to my early childhood, to the hospital grounds where I lived and to an unforgettable moment I experienced there.

For my family to live in hospital housing was quite a common circumstance in China in those days, when the majority of urban employees were housed by their work units. I grew up in a medical environment, roaming idle and alone through the sick wards, lingering in the corridors, dropping in on elderly patients who knew me, asking new inmates what was wrong with them. First, though, I would wander into nurses' stations and grab a few swabs soaked in alcohol to wipe my hands. I didn't have showers very often then,

but I would scrub my fingers with alcohol at least ten times
a day, and for a while I must have had the world's cleanest
pair of hands. Every day too I breathed the smell of Lysol;
many of my classmates loathed its odor, but I liked it and
even had a theory that, since Lysol is a disinfectant, then
breathing its fumes would be good for my lungs. Today I
still find myself favorably disposed toward Lysol, because
that's the smell that surrounded me as I grew up.

My brother and I often played outside the operating
room where my father toiled. Next to it was a large empty
lot where on sunny days laundry was hung out to dry. We
liked to run back and forth among the damp cotton sheets,
letting them slap our faces with their soapy scent.

This memory, though happy, is dotted with bloodstains.
When my father came out of surgery, his smock and face
mask would be covered in blood. A nurse would often
emerge with a bucket—full of bloody bits and pieces cut
from the bodies of his patients—which she would dump
in the adjacent pond. In the summer the pond gave off a
sickening stench, and flies settled on it so thickly one might
think it had been covered with a black wool carpet.

In those days the housing block had no sanitary facilities, just a public toilet across the yard, next to the morgue.
Neither of these structures had a door, and I got into the
habit of taking a peek inside the morgue every time I went
to the toilet. The morgue was spotlessly clean; a concrete
bed lay underneath a little window, through which I saw
leaves swaying. The morgue stands out in my memory as a
place of unimaginable serenity. The tree that grew outside
its window was noticeably greener and more luxuriant than
the others around it, but I do not know if that was because
of the morgue or because of the toilet.

I lived ten years of my life opposite the morgue, and
it's fair to say that I grew up amid the sound of weeping.
Patients who had died would lie in the morgue the night

before their cremation. Like a roadside rest stop where one breaks a long journey, the morgue silently received those time-pressed travelers as they moved from life to death.

Many nights I would suddenly wake from sleep and listen to the desolate wails of those who had lost their loved ones. During those years I must have heard every kind of weeping there is, and the longer the weeping went on, the less it sounded like weeping—especially as dawn approached, when the cries of the bereaved seemed particularly sustained and heartrending. To me those cries conveyed a mysterious intimacy, the intimacy of depthless sorrow, and for a time I thought of them as the most stirring songs I had ever heard. Only later did I learn that it is under cover of night that most people pass away.

In those days there was no relief from the searing heat of summer, and often I would wake from an afternoon nap to find the entire outline of my body imprinted in sweat on my straw bed mat; sometimes I perspired so heavily it bleached my skin white.

One day, when curiosity impelled me to step inside the morgue, it felt as though I had exchanged torrid sunshine for chilly moonlight. Although I had walked past the morgue on countless occasions, this was the first time I had ventured across its threshold, and I was struck by how refreshingly cool it was inside. When I lay down on that clean concrete bed, I found the ideal place for an afternoon nap. On many baking afternoons that followed, if I saw that the morgue was not otherwise occupied, I would lie on the slab and savor its soothing coolness; sometimes in my dreams I would find myself in a garden full of blooming flowers.

Since I grew up in the Cultural Revolution, my education had made me a skeptic in matters of the spirit. Not believing in ghosts, I had no fear of them either. So when I lay down on the slab, it did not carry connotations of death.

What it meant to me was a cool haven, an escape from the sweltering summer.

There were, however, several awkward moments. Sometimes I had just fallen asleep on the slab when I was awoken by cries and screams, and realized that a dead person was about to visit. Hurrying off as the weeping got closer and closer, the concrete bed's temporary occupant made way for its overnight guest.

All this happened a long time ago. Growing up is, in a sense, a process of forgetting, and later in life I completely forgot about this macabre but beautiful childhood moment: how on a stifling-hot summer afternoon I lay in the morgue, on the slab that symbolized death, and there experienced life's cooling caress.

So things remained until one day, many years later, I happened upon a line in a poem by Heine: "Death is the cooling night." That childhood memory, lost for so long, suddenly restored itself to my quivering heart, returning freshly washed, in limpid clarity, never again to leave me.

If literature truly possesses a mysterious power, I think perhaps it is precisely this: that one can read a book by a writer of a different time, a different country, a different race, a different language, and a different culture and there encounter a sensation that is one's very own. Heine put into words the feeling I had as a child when I lay napping in the morgue. And that, I tell myself, is literature.

写作

writing

Pankaj Mishra had been asked to write a piece about me for the *New York Times Magazine* and came to Beijing in November 2008. We spent hours talking together, sometimes in the warmth and comfort of indoors, sometimes venturing outside for a walk in the icy wind. When we ate out, I made a point of introducing him to different regional cuisines, and on his departure my new vegetarian friend complimented me on my skill in selecting dishes. "Well, it's not much of a skill," I told him. "I just order all the vegetarian dishes a restaurant has on its menu."

If Mishra was grateful to me, I too was grateful to him. "To recall one's past life," Martial wrote, "is to relive it." In the space of that short week, Mishra had me revisit my writing career, and thus bestowed on me a life relived.

"My writing° goes back a long way," I told him—such a long way, in fact, that it seems to emanate from another world. When I cast about for examples of my juvenilia, my thoughts skip quickly over my old composition books and gather instead on the big-character posters that were then pasted everywhere. Those primary-school compositions are not worth mentioning, because they had only a single

°*xiezuo*

62

reader, my bespectacled Chinese teacher. I prefer to start with the big-character posters that I authored, for they were the first works of mine to be displayed to the world at large.

In the Cultural Revolution era we were even more passionate about writing big-character posters than people are today about writing blogs. The difference between the two genres is this: The posters tended to be tediously alike, basically just a rehash of articles in the *People's Daily,* their text riddled with revolutionary rhetoric and empty slogans, blathering endlessly on and on. Blogs, on the other hand, take a multitude of forms—self-promoting or abusive, disclosing intimate details here and carried away by righteous indignation there, striking affected poses right and left—and they dwell on every topic under the sun, from society and politics to economics and history and goodness knows what else. But in one respect the two genres are much the same: writing big-character posters during the Cultural Revolution and keeping a blog today are both designed to assert the value of one's own existence.

As a little boy in primary school I was terrified of big-character posters. Every morning as I headed off to class with my satchel on my back I would nervously scan the walls on either side of the street, checking to see if my father's name appeared in the headlines of the latest batch of posters.

My father was a surgeon and a low-level functionary in the Communist Party. In the early stages of the Cultural Revolution I had personally witnessed the disgrace of several of my classmates' fathers who were officials; they were denounced for being "power holders following the capitalist road." Activists in the revolutionary rebel faction beat them till their faces were black-and-blue, and they were forced to wear wooden signs over their chests and tall dunce caps on their heads. I would see them every day with brooms in their hands, trembling with fear as they swept the streets.

Passersby would give them a kick if they felt like it, or spit in their faces. Their children naturally shared the ignominy, being constant butts of their classmates' insults and targets of their discrimination.

I lived on tenterhooks, anxious that my father might suddenly suffer a similarly awful fate, bringing me down with him. What made things worse was that my father had a landlord pedigree, for his family had once owned some thirty acres of land, which defined them as landlords pure and simple. Fortunately my grandfather had been a slacker with no ambitions to improve himself; all he knew how to do was to party and play around, and so every year he would sell off a piece of land here and there to pay for his extravagant lifestyle. By 1949 this wastrel had managed neatly to burn his way through the whole estate, and in so doing he sold off his landlord status. If he had held on to his land, he could hardly have avoided being shot when the country was liberated. So my father reaped the fruits of the family shame, dodging the nasty stigma of being a "landlord's brat." My brother, Hua Xu, and I, needless to say, were equal (though more distant) beneficiaries of my grandfather's spendthrift ways.

Nevertheless, my father's inglorious family history remained a source of anguish for me. Bad things are bound to happen sooner or later, and one morning Hua Xu and I finally saw on the way to school the big-character poster that I had most been dreading. My father's name was emblazoned across the title, accompanied by two condemnatory labels: "runaway landlord" and "capitalist-roader."

I was a fainthearted, fearful boy, and I'm sure my face must have completely paled at the sight of this headline. I told my brother I couldn't summon up the courage to go to school—I was going to stay home and lie low. Hua Xu shrugged the whole thing off, saying there was nothing to worry about, and marched off toward school as though without a care in the world. His nerve held only for a hundred yards or so; at that point he turned around and came marching back. "Damn it, there's no way I'm going to school either," he muttered. "I'm going to lie low, too."

Such was the backdrop to the creation of the first big-character poster to which I ever signed my name. With his life now at such a low ebb, my father chose both to stage and to perform in an exhibition of political theater, one that enabled the entire family to experience the Chinese New Year in full revolutionary style. Other households, having skimped and saved the whole year through, were able to indulge themselves for once in some lavish meat and fish dishes, but our meal instead consisted of "remembering the bitter to think of the sweet." What that meant was mixing rice husks and weeds together and boiling them until soft, then kneading them into dumplings. In the old days "chaff dumplings" had been eaten only by the very poor, and for us to eat them on the most festive evening of the Chinese calendar was to taste the bitterness of the old society and savor the sweetness of the new.

I held one of these chaff dumplings with two hands and nibbled it cautiously. It was bland and tasteless, but I could feel the coarse husks scratching my throat as I swallowed. It hurt to eat them, and I told my parents so. My father put the best possible face on this. "It's good if it hurts," he assured me in a doctor's upbeat tone. "That just shows you're seeing the benefits of remembering the bitter to think of the sweet."

My brother and I didn't realize that our father, in his misfortune, was performing a revolutionary show, for which he had selected this ideal occasion of New Year's Eve. A few days later, in the confessional materials that he submitted to his inquisitors, he made a great song and dance about this revolutionized Spring Festival, as a way of expressing his boundless loyalty to Mao Zedong and the Communist Party.

After we had all swallowed our chaff dumplings and my mother had cleared away the dishes, my father spread open a huge sheet of paper, bigger even than the table, and we set to work writing a big-character poster. "Denounce the selfish and criticize the revisionist"—such was the theme of the hour. "Tonight, this last day of the year," my father told us gravely as he ground ink in the ink stone, "we must do a thorough job of criticism and self-criticism."

Hua Xu and I found this prospect invigorating and were both eager to be the first to address the topic. Neither of us was willing to yield ground to the other, so determined were we to demonstrate our prowess in self-criticism. My parents said I should go first: my brother, being two years older, ought to allow me this opportunity to shine. But, blinking desperately, I found myself unable on the spur of the moment to quite put a finger on my selfish, revisionist thinking. As I hesitated, Hua Xu restively pressed to speak, only to be overruled by my parents. They began to coach me, telling me that a few minutes earlier, when I felt that my throat was sore, that was actually selfish thought rearing its head. This took a big weight off my mind, but I still felt anxious. "Could that count as revisionist thought, too?" I asked.

My parents conferred. This did seem to be undoubted evidence of petit bourgeois attitudes muddling my mind, and bourgeois rubbish was a sure sign of revisionism. They nodded. "Yes, it counts."

So, selfishness and revisionism—it was all there. I could breathe easily at last. Now it was Hua Xu's turn. He announced proudly that he had once found a two-fen coin in the street but failed to hand it in to the teacher, instead buying himself two pieces of candy. My parents nodded solemnly. This act of my brother's, they declared, was very similar to mine, an error that combined both selfishness and revisionism. Next up was my mother, and after her effort to combat selfishness and criticize revisionism it was my father's turn. Our parents mentioned only a few peccadillos that were neither here nor there, leaving Hua Xu and me quite disappointed. My father's performance was a particular letdown, for his self-criticism made no mention of being a runaway landlord and a capitalist-roader. My brother at once challenged him on this score. "Are you a runaway landlord?" he asked sternly.

My father, stone-faced, shook his head. The family had lost all its property before Liberation, he said, and during land reform they were classified as middle peasants. Why, if not for those thirty acres they had once owned, my mother chimed in, they would have ended up as poor peasants. Hua Xu raised his right hand gravely. "Can you swear to Chairman Mao that you're not a landlord?"

My father raised his hand with equal gravity. "I swear to Chairman Mao, I am not a landlord."

I wanted a share of the action, too. "Well, are you a revisionist?" I asked.

Again he shook his head. It was true he had joined the party before Liberation, he said, but all these years he had been engaged purely in technical work—a surgeon all along—so he didn't count as a power holder pursuing the capitalist road.

Following Hua Xu's cue, I raised my hand. "Can you swear to Chairman Mao?"

Again he raised his hand. "I swear to Chairman Mao."

Then we watched as he wrote the big-character poster. It skimmed over major issues and dwelled only on trivia, but it was our first effort at self-criticism, written on the eve of the Chinese New Year, no less. My father signed his name at the end, then proffered the brush to my mother, who signed her name and passed it on to my brother. I added my name at the very bottom.

Next we began to discuss where to display our poster.

Let's put it outside our front door, I said—that way the neighbors can admire our New Year's Eve accomplishment. No, it should go up next to the cinema box office, Hua Xu argued—big-character posters had more readers there. Our parents must surely have been inwardly cursing us little devils, because for them this was purely a show, designed to display their revolutionary spirit and political awareness; they had not the slightest desire to have others view the poster. Moreover, this New Year's Eve poster had considerable practical value, providing material for a splendid passage in my father's exculpatory statement.

However dismayed our parents may have been to hear our suggestions, they simulated a warm sympathy for them, nodding vigorously and commending our initiative but pointing out that there was a problem with putting the poster up outside, for this would make it impossible for us to see it at all times. We ourselves were the objects of criticism in this poster, they explained patiently, so it should be placed on view in our own house, alerting us constantly to our past errors and ensuring that in the future we would always stick closely to Chairman Mao and travel far on the correct path.

In those days we had not yet moved to the hospital dormitory and lived in a house in a little street named Sunnyside Lane. It was one big room, divided into two by a partition made from a bamboo lattice over which old newspapers were pasted. My parents slept in the inner sanctum, while my brother and I shared a bed by the door. We felt they had a point and agreed to put up the poster inside the house, but we insisted on one thing: it must be stuck at the head of our bed, not theirs. This was a condition to which they happily consented.

Not long afterward my father was sent down to the countryside. With a medicine chest on his back he roamed from village to village, dispensing medical care to the peasants.

By the time the rebel faction realized they had let him slip from their grasp and sent people to fetch him back, he was nowhere to be found. The simple country folk had hidden him for his protection, and so by great good fortune he avoided the revolutionary violence of the early stages of the Cultural Revolution.

That glorious poster maintained its position above our bed for a good year or more, but as it gathered dust and its paper yellowed and tore, it slipped down the wall and under the bed, where we forgot all about it. At the beginning, however, the last thing I did before I went to bed and the first thing I did after I woke up was to look with awe at my spindly signature at the bottom of the poster.

Five years later I entered middle school and there began to write big-character posters on a large scale; this time I wrote them myself and didn't just append my signature at the end. In the Cultural Revolution the most illustrious writing group came from two universities: Peking and Tsing-hua. Its nom de plume was Liang Xiao, a play on words for "Two Schools." In imitation of Liang Xiao, I recruited three classmates to form a writing team that took its name from a famous film of the period called *Spring Shoots*.

This was when the Huang Shuai incident was making headlines all over the country. Huang Shuai, a twelve-year-old, had criticized a teacher in her diary. She wrote:

Today XX did not observe classroom protocol and caused some disruption. Teacher called him to the front. "I really feel like giving you a good whack on the head with my pointer," he told him. That's not the right thing to say, is it? A pointer is to be used for teaching purposes, not to hit pupils over the head with. I hope you will patiently correct students if they make mistakes and be more careful about what you say in the future.

When the teacher saw the diary, he hit the roof, convinced the girl was bent on undermining his authority. In the weeks that followed he subjected Huang Shuai to constant criticism and told her classmates they should have nothing to do with her. Lonely and forlorn, she resorted to writing a two-page letter to the *Beijing Daily*. She protested:

> I am a junior Red Guard who loves the party and Chairman Mao. All I did was write what I thought in my diary, but the teacher just won't let it go. For so many days now I have been unable to eat, and when I try to sleep, I have nightmares that make me cry. Just what is this terrible mistake I have committed? Surely we young people in the age of Mao Zedong can't be expected to be slaves to the oppressive old educational system with its notions of "teacher's dignity"!

In mid-December 1973 the *Beijing Daily* published Huang Shuai's letter and excerpts from her diary. Later that month the *People's Daily* reprinted the whole article as the top lead on the front page, adding an editorial comment for good measure. The Central People's Broadcasting Service reported the story, too. Huang Shuai was a celebrity for a time, an anti-establishment hero and role model to students all over the country. But good times don't last. Three years later, with the death of Mao and the fall of Madame Mao and her cronies, Huang Shuai fell from heaven into hell, labeled at sixteen a lackey of the Gang of Four.* Big-character posters criticizing her sprouted up

---

*Gang of Four was the name given to a radical faction influential in the latter stages of the Cultural Revolution, consisting of Jiang Qing, Zhang Chunqiao, Yao Wenyuan, and Wang Hongwen. Removed from office in October 1976, they were subsequently jailed. The campaign against the authority of teachers served a radical agenda by counteracting the efforts of Zhou Enlai and others to restore order to the educational system.

everywhere, and her parents came to grief as well. Her mother wrote a long self-denunciation, and her father was arrested, emerging with his name cleared only in 1981. In that era, destiny did not rest in one's own hands; everyone found himself swept along in the current, and nobody knew whether fortune or fiasco lay ahead.

In late 1973, as the campaign to criticize "teacher's dignity" swept through Chinese schools, the big-character posters I wrote under the name of Spring Shoots caused quite a stir in my school and I enjoyed a fleeting reputation as a "red pen." Red being the color of revolution and black the color of counterrevolution, a "red pen" was a politically correct author, in contradistinction to the "black pen," purveyor of politically suspect works.

Three classmates and I wielded our brushes energetically in round-the-clock writing sessions, copying revolutionary phrases verbatim from the *People's Daily, Zhejiang Daily,* and Shanghai's *Liberation Daily.* Before the week was out we had completed close to forty big-character posters, which we plastered over the walls of our school. In them we fiercely criticized every member of the teaching staff, with one exception: the teacher of Chinese, with whom I had quite a good relationship. He would often slip me a cigarette, and every time I swiped a few cigs from my father I would make sure to repay his generosity.

In those days the working class was the leader in all things, and in every work unit (except for factories, military bases, and rural villages) a workers' propaganda team had been installed. When one of these teams moved into our school, its leader became, in effect, the top administrator. He was a worker in his fifties, and as he perused our posters he scribbled away in his notebook and greeted me with a smile. "Good job! Good job!" he enthused.

Little did I realize that those forty posters our Spring Shoots group had cooked up served to bolster his revolutionary credentials. The chairman of the county revolutionary committee heaped praise on him, declaring that our school was in the top rank of schools in our county in its dedication to the movement to emulate Huang Shuai's anti-establishment spirit and critique teacher's dignity and might indeed be among the top schools in the entire province.

The workers'-propaganda team leader earnestly recorded the names of all the teachers we had criticized, only to discover that the teacher of Chinese had been overlooked. He was not at all happy about that, for this revealed a blind spot in the campaign. He summoned the blind spot to his office and there banged on the desk and burst into a stream of expletives, expounding his belief that the only thing that could possibly explain the absence of criticism was that this blind spot was oppressing and mistreating his students.

Our teacher sought me out, grim-faced. He led me to a secluded corner beyond the school walls and handed me a cigarette, which he lit with a match. "Why didn't you write a poster about me?" he asked plaintively.

I sucked on my cigarette. "You've got no shred of teacher's dignity," I told him.

"How can that be?" He became agitated. "Teacher's dignity—I'm dignified from head to toe!"

"You're always giving us cigarettes," I objected. "You treat us on an equal basis. I don't see that you have any teacher's dignity at all."

He didn't know whether to laugh or cry and had no choice but to tell me about his harrowing interview with the propaganda team leader. Now I understood. I promised I'd get a poster criticizing him done that very evening and he'd see it as soon he got up in the morning.

I was as good as my word. After dinner I summoned my writing-group partners, and we wrote away in the classroom until late that night. We had allotted one poster each to the other instructors, but we went one better with the teacher of Chinese and wrote two full posters about him. Then, clutching the posters, we went to his home, and as he slept soundly inside we conferred about where to stick them up. Originally I thought we would stick them to his door, but there wasn't room there for both of them, so the best we could do was post one on each side.

The following morning the teacher ushered me once more to a quiet spot outside the school—not to thank me, as I was expecting, but to lodge a complaint. I shouldn't have stuck the posters outside his door, he said, for the propaganda team leader would never see them there, and they would just make him a laughingstock among the neighbors. Much better to stick a poster up right outside the team leader's office. Seeing me nod, he raised another sore point: why did I have to write two posters about him when one was good enough for the others? Well, that was to elevate him to a higher category, I told him.

"No, no, I don't want to be higher than anyone else," he said. "Equal treatment—that's all I want."

"All right, then," I agreed. "We'll go the extra mile and write a new poster for you."

"What about the ones outside my door?" he asked.

"Just tear them down when you get home."

"How could I dare do that?" the teacher practically howled. "You come take them down yourself," he whispered.

Then he coached me on what to say when I came at lunchtime to carry out this mission. I nodded and reassured him that everything would be done just as he instructed. He groped around in his pocket, brought out a half-empty pack of cigarettes, and handed me one. He took a few steps, then stopped, turned around, and gave me the rest of the pack.

As promised, I finished writing the poster before the end of the morning session and posted it outside the team leader's office. Then my associates and I marched over to the teacher's house, shouting his name outside his door. He deliberately lingered inside and failed to emerge, and only after the neighbors had rushed out to watch the excitement did he venture forth, bowing and scraping. "Listen up!" I scolded. "We've written another poster about your teacher's dignity, an even more powerful critique than these two here, and we put it up in the school. Go and read it right away!"

He trotted off obediently toward the school. We made a great show of tearing down the posters outside his house, explaining to the neighbors that they lacked sufficient depth, not like the newly written poster stuck up in the school, which we welcomed them to read.

In my final years in high school I continued to write, but I suddenly lost interest in big-character posters. Instead I tried writing a play, which I suppose counts as my first literary work. I must have spent the best part of one semester writing a one-act play, about nine or ten pages long. I revised it several times, then copied it out carefully onto squared writing paper. Its subject matter was very popular at the time: a landlord, having seen all his property confiscated after Liberation, was bitterly resentful and tried to sabotage socialist reconstruction in the countryside but was caught in the act by the clever and resourceful poor and lower-middle peasants.

In our town there lived a well-known red pen, quite a bit older than me, who had made a name for himself by publishing a great many poems and essays extolling the Cultural Revolution in the mimeographed magazine of the local cultural center. Through a classmate's good offices I managed to make the acquaintance of this small-town celebrity, and I respectfully presented him with a copy of my play and invited his comments.

A few days later, when I went to visit him for the second

time, he had read my play and had also written a lengthy paragraph of comments in red ink on the final page. He returned the manuscript to me with a very self-important air. I'd find his comments at the end, he said, and there was nothing much to add, except for one point he wanted to emphasize: there was no psychology in my play—no soliloquies, in other words. Soliloquies, he informed me, were the sine qua non of playwriting.

I was about to take my leave when he brought out a three-act play that he had recently completed. It dealt with the same kind of story as my own: a landlord bent on sabotage, only to be apprehended by poor and lower-middle peasants. As he thrust the bulky manuscript into my hands he asked me to pay special attention to how he handled soliloquies. "Particularly the landlord's soliloquies," he preened. "They're so graphic."

I carried both manuscripts home. First I carefully read his comments on my play. They were all criticisms, basically, apart from a few words of praise at the end, when he said I wrote smoothly enough. Then I carefully read his play. I couldn't see what was so great about it either; those landlord's soliloquies of which he was so proud were merely formulaic phrases in which the landlord talked about how he intended to wreak havoc on socialism, and the graphic language consisted simply of some dirty words with which his remarks were interlarded. Such were the standard conventions of the time: workers and peasants never used swearwords; bad language was the preserve of landlords, rightists, and counterrevolutionaries. I felt, nonetheless, that I ought to compliment him, for he was somebody of considerable stature in our town. I paid him a reciprocal courtesy, fetching a red pen and writing a long paragraph of comments in the blank space on the final page. My comments were basically all favorable, and I waxed especially lyrical when it came to the landlord's soliloquies, which I praised to the skies, saying that such brilliant writing really had no match in the world. Only at the very end did I add a criticism to the effect that the organization was a bit loose.

When I returned his manuscript, I could tell from the look in his eyes that he was looking forward to my puffery and adulation. I made a number of flattering remarks that made him chuckle. Then suddenly he was in a fury—he had noticed my commentary on the last page. "You dare to write something on my manuscript?" he roared.

I was taken by surprise, never having imagined that my reciprocity would provoke such anger. "You wrote on my manuscript, too," I protested timidly.

"What the fuck!" he shouted. "Who do you think you are? Who do you think I am?"

He had a point. He was a name and I was a nobody. Seeing the criticism that ended my commentary, he flew into a towering rage. "You're way too big for your boots!" he cried, giving me a kick. "You have the gall to tell me the organization is loose?"

I hurriedly retreated a couple of paces and pointed out that there were many respectful comments as well. He bent his head to read more closely, and when he saw how I fawned over his landlord's soliloquies, his anger visibly subsided. He sat down in a chair and had me sit down, too. After reading my comments through from start to finish, he seemed to recover his composure. He did, however, start grumbling that my having written in red pen made it impossible to give the script to anybody else to read. I suggested he tear out the last page and rewrite the ending on a new sheet of paper—I even offered to do the recopying. He waved his hand to decline. "Forget it, I'll do it myself."

A smile of contentment began to appear on his face. Two officials from the cultural center had read his play, he confided, and they were tremendously impressed; there was a veritable flood of good reviews. I remained skeptical. How could the reaction of two people be called "a flood of good reviews," I wondered. But I feigned delight nonetheless. The workers'-propaganda team leader at the county cultural center was currently reviewing the play, he went on. As soon as it was given the all-clear, the county Mao Zedong Thought Publicity Team would start rehearsals; after five nights at the county playhouse the play would move to the provincial capital and compete in the Popular Arts Festival.

The small-town big shot's complacency continued for a few more days before his career took a nosedive. The propaganda team leader at the cultural center was an uncultured boor whose education had ended at primary school. After reading the landlord's soliloquies, he came to the conclusion that their author must be a counterrevolutionary bent on sabotaging socialist reconstruction. To him the landlord's soliloquies were nothing more and nothing less than the author's soliloquies.

The playwright found this most unjust. Those soliloquies were the landlord's, he explained; they weren't his. The propaganda team leader tapped the bulging manuscript. "These words in the mind of the landlord—are they your work?"

"That's right," he said, "but—"

"If that's what you write, that's what you think." The team leader would hear nothing more.

Our local celebrity changed overnight from a red pen to a black one. In the two years that followed he would often make appearances on the stage in the high school playing field where public sentencing rallies were conducted. There he would play the role of an "active counterrevolutionary," a big wooden sign over his chest, head bowed, his whole body shaking with terror. Every time I saw him there I would feel a chill at the back of my neck and think to myself what a close shave I'd had. How lucky for me that the landlord in my play had no soliloquy and that my comments at the end of his play had been excised, otherwise a place might have been made for me next to him on the stage.

In those days sentencing rallies would be held in the high school playing field several times each year, to publicly announce the sentence on one or several murderers, rapists, and other offenders. On each occasion a number of landlords, rightists, and counterrevolutionaries would be brought in to serve as supplementary targets. Unbound but with big wooden signs hanging over their chests, they would flank the major offenders, who were trussed up like chickens. Not every landlord, rightist, and counterrevolutionary would participate in every supplementary struggle event, but the playwright was an exception, perhaps because he was so well-known. Every time there was a public sentencing he would appear with his head bowed, placard on his chest, occupying a fixed position on the far right. He was our town's default accessory target.

A few years later my parents worried themselves sick when I began to write fiction in earnest. Their experiences during the Cultural Revolution gave them cause to fear that their son one day might end up as just another black pen.

Pankaj Mishra's eyes gleamed. A wise listener, he smiles quietly and, when he laughs, laughs quietly, too. We were fishers of memory, sitting on the banks of time and waiting for the past to swallow the bait.

The conversation turned to my first career, as a dentist, and my second career, as a writer. Thirty years ago I was working away with my forceps in a small-town hospital, extracting teeth for eight hours a day. From morning to night my job consisted of looking inside people's gaping mouths, places where you are guaranteed to find the world's least attractive scenery. In my five years of dentistry, I told Mishra, I must have extracted more than ten thousand teeth.

I had just turned twenty then, and during my lunch

break I would stand by a window overlooking the street and watch all the bustle below, with a terrifying thought running through my head: I couldn't spend my whole life doing this, could I? That was when I decided to be an author.

From my window I would often see people from the cultural center loafing about on the main street at all hours of the day, and I was green with envy. "Hey, why aren't you working?" I asked one of them.

"Walking the street, that is our work," he replied.

That's the kind of work I would like to do, I thought. Apart from heaven itself, where else but the cultural center could one find such a cushy job? In China then, individuals had no power to choose their own career: all employment was assigned by the state. After my graduation from high school the state made me be a dentist. For me now to abandon dental work for a loafer's life in the cultural center required the state's permission, and for that to happen I had, above all, to demonstrate that I was qualified to make the switch. There were three routes of access to the cultural center: you could be a composer, you could be a painter, or you could be a writer. To compose music or paint pictures, I would have had to learn everything from scratch, so they posed too much of a challenge; writing just required knowledge of Chinese characters, so for me it was the only option.

I completed my primary and secondary education during the ten years of the Cultural Revolution, which made for rich experience as I was growing up but also meant that proper study went by the wayside. In high school I would often confuse the bell for the start of a period with the bell that marked its end, and go into class just after it had finished. At the time I knew only a limited stock of Chinese characters, although they served me well enough in my own writing. Years later, when Chinese critics were unanimous in praising my plain narrative language, I would laugh it off: "That's because I don't know so many characters."

When my work was translated into English, a literature professor in the United States told me that my style
reminded him of Hemingway, giving me a chance to recycle
my joke. "He can't have had much of a vocabulary either,"
I said.

Though I was being facetious, there was some truth
there, too. Life is often this way: you may start off with an
advantage, only to box yourself in over time, or sometimes
you may start with a handicap, only to find it carries you a
long way. Or, as Mao put it, "Good things can become bad,
and bad things can become good." Perhaps Hemingway and
I both fit that model of bad things becoming good.

At the age of twenty-two I went on pulling teeth and also
began to write. The tooth-pulling was to make a living, and
the writing was to get out of having to pull more teeth. At
first writing actually felt the more arduous of the two activities. But in order to reach cultural-center nirvana, I forced
myself to continue. I was young then, and it was no easy
matter to persuade my bottom to maintain such constant
intimacy with my chair. Outside, on weekends, the sunshine
was so enticing, birds were flitting to and fro, girls were
laughing so sweetly, friends my age were gadding about, but
I sat stiffly at my desk, expending as much energy on getting
words out on paper as a blacksmith does beating iron into
shape on his anvil.

Years later young people often ask, "How does one become
a writer?" My answer is always simply: "By writing." Writing
is like experience: if you don't experience things, then you
won't understand life; and if you don't write, then you won't
know what you're capable of creating.

I have fond memories of the early 1980s. The Cultural
Revolution had just finished; magazines that had been
banned for ten years were reappearing, and even more new
magazines were emerging. A China that had hardly any literary journals suddenly became a China with more than a

thousand literary journals. Like hungry babies wailing for milk, a whole array of fiction columns required nourishment. Previously published authors, whether famous or not, could not possibly satisfy the needs of so many publications even if they were to send in all the things they'd written. And so editors were conscientiously reading unsolicited manuscripts; as soon as they stumbled on something good, they would pass it around among themselves, and the whole editorial department would get excited.

It was my good fortune to find myself in this wonderful period when supply and demand were so out of synch. A dentist in a small town, I had no connections with any editors and knew only the addresses of their publications, so I sent my short stories out to journal after journal. In those days one didn't need to pay for postage; instead one simply cut off a corner of the envelope to indicate that the journal would pick up the tab. What's more, if a journal decided not to use a story of mine, it would return the manuscript. After I received a rejected manuscript, I would immediately open the envelope, turn it inside out, glue it closed, write the address of a different journal on top, and chuck it into the mailbox—not forgetting, of course, to snip off a corner.

Manuscripts of my stories traveled for free among the various cities of China; they returned to me again and again, and again and again I sent them on their way once more. They must have traveled to even more cities than I would end up visiting myself in the twenty years that followed. We were living then in a house with a small courtyard, and the mailman would simply toss returned manuscripts over the wall. They would hit the ground with a recognizably heavy thump, and my father, inside the house, had no need to step outside to know what had just been delivered. I would hear my name called, followed by a loud "Reject!"

Before long the relationship of supply and demand between literary works and publishing venues moved in a very different direction. As famous and not-yet-famous authors proliferated like flowers in the spring, literary journals were no longer starving infants; in the blink of an eye they became beautiful young ladies, the objects of fervent courtship and intense rivalry. And as literature itself began to slip from its high perch, the wonderful moment proved ephemeral. Publishers could no longer bear the crippling postage costs, and magazines issued announcements to the effect that (a) authors had to put stamps on their submissions and (b) journals would no longer return manuscripts.

Beijing Literature was the first magazine whose editorial offices I ever visited: a large room lined with desks piled high with submissions from unheralded authors, where the editors sat, quietly reading manuscripts. I noticed how the editors opened envelopes with scissors and studied their contents with great attention. At that point I had yet to publish any of my own work. When I had occasion to visit other magazines' editorial offices the year after several of my stories had appeared in print, I encountered a very different spectacle. The incoming envelopes on the tables were all addressed to individual editors and sent by authors known to them. Piles of manuscripts sent by unknown writers lay unopened in wastepaper baskets, waiting for recycling agents to come and pick them up, for they were being sold off as scrap, to be pulped in the paper mill and made into more writing paper. I realized then that editors were no longer bothering with unsolicited submissions.

From that point on a young writer, however gifted, no matter how excellent his work, would find it extremely difficult to get published if he was not personally acquainted with an editor. This cruel reality remained in place for many years, until the emergence in China of Internet literature, when a new form of publication allowed talented young authors to break through once again.

Looking back, I rejoice that I was able to catch the tail end of that honeymoon period of the early '80s. If I had started writing a couple of years later, I think it very unlikely that an editor would have discovered me in those mountains of unsolicited submissions, and I'd still be there in that small-town hospital in the south, brandishing my forceps and extracting teeth for eight hours a day.

I owe the change in my destiny to a telephone call in November 1983. Winter had come to my little town of Haiyan, and I was just about to knock off for the day when a distant call tracked me down. At the time our hospital had just one single telephone, by the registration desk downstairs. It was a traditional dial telephone, and you needed to route calls through the county's sole telephone exchange in the county post-and-telecommunications office. When my colleague at registration received the call, she ran into the street and yelled my name outside the window of the room where I worked.

As I walked down the stairs I thought it would be one of my friends in the area, setting up a time to play poker or something that evening. But when I picked up the receiver, I heard the voice of the operator in the local telecom office: she told me I had a long-distance call from Beijing. My heart pounded wildly, and I had the feeling that something momentous was about to happen.

In those days one had to wait for some time before a connection was completed, and when I was told there was a call coming in from Beijing, I reckoned it had got no farther than Shanghai and knew it might well encounter further delays before it reached my little town. I ended up having to wait a good half hour, and as I waited so hopefully and impatiently I found it maddening that calls kept coming in for other colleagues. "You're not to complete this call," I would tell the callers with all the authority I could muster.

"Why not?" a mystified voice would respond.

"I'm expecting a call from the Politburo," I would tell them.

Finally the connection was made, and I heard the voice of Zhou Yanru, then executive editor of *Beijing Literature.* The first thing she told me was that she had placed the call as soon as she arrived at her office that morning and it had taken all day to get through. "I had given up hope," she said, "and was ready to start all over again tomorrow."

I'll never forget that conversation. She did not speak quickly, but I felt there was an urgency in her tone and a clarity and correctness to her language. They planned to publish all three stories I had submitted, she said, but one of them needed revision and she wanted me to go to Beijing at once to attend to it. *Beijing Literature* would pick up the tab for my train fare and accommodation—the issue that was of greatest concern to me, since my monthly salary at the time was only 36 yuan. Then she told me I would receive a stipend for each day I spent revising the manuscript, and finally she gave me her office address—7 West Chang'an Avenue—and instructed me to take the No. 10 bus when I got out of the train station. She had no way of knowing that this would be my first trip of any significant distance but went over these details carefully nonetheless, as though coaching a child.

As soon as I put down the phone, I decided to take a bus to Shanghai the following day and then a train from there to Beijing. But immediately I ran into a problem: how to secure a leave of absence from the hospital director? I thought it very likely that he would not agree to let me go, since he had no idea I was writing stories. For a tooth puller to need suddenly to go to Beijing to revise his work—what a preposterous notion! I couldn't afford to approach him directly about it.

That evening I knocked on the door of a fellow dentist

and gave him my leave request, asking him to pass it on to the hospital director when he went to work the following morning. By that time I would already be on the bus to Shanghai; even if the director refused to give me clearance, it would be too late, for the chicken would have flown the coop.

But this colleague of mine proved reluctant to accept the commission, fearing that it might get him into trouble. It was my job to get things squared away, he kept repeating. On my return, I countered, I would present him with a box of Beijing's famous dried fruit and a packet of the biscuits that Empress Dowager Cixi had most adored. Hearing this, my colleague couldn't help but drool, for these things at the time were gourmet items on everybody's wish list. Prudence was no match for temptation: he agreed to wait till I was safely on the bus, then drop off the request. My scheme had succeeded through bribery, we would say today—or through a sugar-coated bullet, as we would have put it then.

The day I entered the editorial offices of *Beijing Literature,* the staff were having their lunch break. Wang Jie (the editor who had discovered me in a huge pile of unsolicited manuscripts) sat me down on a shabby old sofa, poured me a cup of tea, and slipped out. A moment later an old lady with a ruddy complexion pushed open the door. "You're Yu Hua?" she said.

This was Zhou Yanru. She asked me to change the ending to my story, for it was rather bleak and she wanted things to end happily. She who had never seen capitalism told me, who had never seen capitalism either, "Socialism is bright. Only capitalism can be so dark and dismal."

I revised the manuscript in two days, following her instructions to the letter. To me at the time, getting published was more important than anything else. Never mind creating an upbeat ending—if she had asked me to make the whole story sparkle with light from start to finish, I would have put up no resistance. Zhou Yanru, very pleased, complimented me on my cleverness, then told me not to rush home. I should have a good look around the capital while I was there.

At that time I had no idea I would later make my home in Beijing, so I felt this was a priceless opportunity and roamed everywhere, trying to take in all the sights. China's tourist industry was still in its infancy then, and during my whole time in the Forbidden City I saw only a dozen or so sightseers—such a contrast with today, when visiting a heritage site feels more like attending a mass rally. I took a long-haul bus to the Great Wall and climbed the steep slope at Badaling. There the bitter wind from Mongolia blew so hard it felt like several hands slapping me on the face over and over again. I met only one other tourist on the Great Wall: as I climbed up toward the beacon tower he was coming down. I greeted him and suggested he join me on another climb, but he shook his head vigorously. "Way too cold," he said with a shiver.

When I descended and entered the run-down little bus station, the tourist I had just seen was huddled in a corner, still shivering. There was no sign of the bus that would take us back to the city, so I sat down next to him and began shivering, too.

After all my excursions I asked Wang Jie where else was worth seeing. She mentioned a few places; I said I had been to them all. "Time to go home, then," she said with a smile. She went off and bought my train ticket, sat at the desk and totted up my expenses, then went to the business office to collect my money. I discovered then that not only would the two days I'd spent revising my manuscript be reimbursed but the days I'd spent sightseeing would be, too. When I traveled back south on the train, I had more than 70 yuan in my pocket, a princely sum to me at the time, and it gave me an unabashed sensation that I was the richest person in the world.

Wang Jie also provided written confirmation that I had revised a manuscript for *Beijing Literature*. It was not until I was back in Haiyan that I realized the importance of this document, for the first thing that the hospital director said to me when he saw me was: "Do you have any proof?"

I came back to find my little town all in a tizzy, for I must have been the first person in the history of our district to have been summoned to Beijing to make revisions to a manuscript. The local officials came to the conclusion that I must be some kind of genius, and they said they could not have me go on extracting teeth but should put me to work in the cultural center. That's how, after a complex transfer procedure, with seven or eight red seals of approval stamped on my papers, I finally gained entry to the cultural center that I had dreamed of for so long. On my first day of work I made a point of showing up two hours late, only to discover I was the first to arrive. I knew then this was just the place for me.

That is my most beautiful memory of socialism.

A few years ago a Western reporter asked me why I abandoned the profitable world of dentistry for a writer's paltry income. What he didn't realize is that China at the time had just started to initiate reforms, and it was still the era of socialist egalitarianism—everyone eating from the same big pot. All employees in cities and towns got paid exactly the same, no matter what kind of work they were engaged in. I was a pauper in the cultural center, but I had been a pauper as a dentist, too. The difference was that a dentist was a pauper mired in drudgery, whereas now I was a pauper who enjoyed freedom and fulfillment.

Many years have passed since then, but my love of writing remains undiminished. All of us have countless desires and emotions that we cannot express, inhibited as we are by mundane realities and rational instincts. But in the world of writing these suppressed desires and emotions can find an unrestricted outlet. Writing tends to promote physical and psychological health, I feel, for it can make one's life complete. To put it another way, writing enables me to claim ownership of two lives, one imaginary and one real, and the relationship between them is like that between sickness and health: when one is strong, the other is bound to fall into decline. So, as my real life becomes more routine, my imaginary life is all the more brimming with incident.

After his visit to Beijing, Pankaj Mishra sent me an e-mail, perhaps from his home in London, perhaps from his home in New Delhi, or perhaps from some corner of the world that I have never heard of. "Why is it that your early short stories are so full of blood and violence," he asked, "when this tendency is not so evident in your later work?"

It's not easy to respond to this kind of query, not because it has no answer but because it has too many. Mishra, as a novelist himself, must know I could offer any number of reasons. I could talk eloquently on the subject for days on end, until my tongue was sore, only to find there was still more to say, yet more answers clamoring for attention. Experience tells me that too many answers are the same as none at all; perhaps only one can constitute a real answer. So I will supply just a single explanation, one that I think may be the most important; whether it is the true answer is impossible to know.

It's your experience while growing up, I believe, that shapes the direction of your life. A basic image of the world is planted deep in your mind, and then, like a document in a copy machine, it keeps being reprinted again and again throughout your formative years. Once you reach adulthood, whether you're successful or not, whatever you accomplish can only partially revise that most basic image; it will never be entirely transformed. Naturally some revise the image more and some revise it less. Mao Zedong, I'm sure, made more revisions than I have done.

It's my conviction that the bloodshed and mayhem of my work in the 1980s were shaped by my experiences as a child. I was just entering primary school when the Cultural Revolution began, and I had just graduated from high school when it ended. In my early years I witnessed countless rallies, denunciation sessions, and battles between rebel factions, not to mention a constant stream of street fights. For me it was a regular occurrence to walk down a street lined with big-character posters and run into people with blood streaming down their faces. That was the larger context of my childhood, and the smaller context was equally bloody. My brother and I were used to running around in hospital corridors and patient wards, inured to screams and sobs, to pallid faces and last gasps, to blood-soaked gauze tossed on the floors of sickrooms and hallways. Sometimes, if the nurse had stepped away from her station outside the surgery door, we would quickly slip in, unchallenged, to observe an operation. We watched, entranced, as our father, wearing transparent gloves, slipped his hands through the abdominal incision and rummaged around in the patient's organs and intestines. "Get out of here!" he would yell when he discovered us, and we would scamper away.

From 1986 to 1989 was my peak period for writing about blood and violence. In one of his books the critic Hong Zhigang lists eight stories I wrote during these years and comes up with no fewer than twenty-nine characters who die unnatural deaths within their pages. During the day as I worked on my stories, there were bound to be gruesome slayings and people dying in pools of blood. At night as I slept, I would dream I was being hunted down and killed. In those nightmares I would find myself friendless and alone, and when I wasn't searching frantically for a hiding place, I'd be desperately fleeing down a highway. Typically, just as I was about to come to a bad end—as an axe was about to sever my neck, for example—I would awake with a start, dripping with sweat, my heart pounding, and it would take me a minute to pull myself together. "Thank God that was just a dream!" I would cry with relief.

But at daybreak, when I sat down at my desk and began to write, it was as though I had forgotten all about my night-time trauma, and what poured forth from my pen was yet more bloodshed and violence. A new cycle of retribution would commence, and at night when I slept I would dream once again that I was on somebody's death list. Life in those three years was so frenzied and so hideous: by day I would kill people in fiction, and by night I would be hunted down in dreams. As this pattern went on repeating itself I worked myself to the edge of nervous collapse but continued heedlessly to immerse myself in the agitation of writing, a creative high that took its own toll.

This went on until one night when I had a very protracted dream. Unlike the other nightmares, from which I always awoke before the moment of death, in this one I experienced my own annihilation. Perhaps I was just so tired that day that the prospect of my death failed to frighten me awake. It was this prolonged nightmare that enabled me to recover a true memory.

Let me say more about this memory. Although there was no shortage of violence during the Cultural Revolution, small-town life was basically very dull and confining. So whenever an execution took place, the little town on Hang-zhou Bay where I grew up would buzz with excitement, as though it were a public holiday. Trials at the time, as I have noted, culminated in a sentencing rally on the high school playing field. The prisoners awaiting punishment stood at the front of the stage with a big sign on their chests identifying their crime: COUNTERREVOLUTIONARY/MURDERER, RAPIST/MURDERER, ROBBER/MURDERER, and so forth. Behind them sat the members of the county revolutionary committee. On either side were arrayed the ancillary targets of struggle, like landlords and rightists, "historical" counterrevolutionaries and "active" counterrevolutionaries. The convicted prisoners stood, heads bowed, as a representative of the revolutionary committee delivered into the microphone an impassioned indictment of their crimes and announced their sentences. If an offender was trussed up and had two armed guards towering over him, this meant he was earmarked for execution.

From my early childhood, I witnessed one after another of these rallies. Squeezed among the crowd of townspeople who packed the playing field, I would listen to the strident harangues that blared from the loudspeaker. The judgment took the form of a prolonged critique, starting off with sayings of Mao Zedong and quotations from Lu Xun, followed by paragraphs consisting largely of boilerplate borrowed from the *People's Daily,* verbose and flavorless. My legs would be aching when I finally heard what crime the person had committed. The sentence itself was brief and to the point, consisting of just five words: "Sentenced to death, execution immediate!"

There were no courts in China during the Cultural Revolution, nor any appeals after sentencing, and we had never in our lives heard of such a thing as the legal profession. After the penalty was announced, there was no chance of lodging an appeal. Prisoners were taken directly to the execution ground and shot.

When the words "Sentenced to death, execution immediate" were read out, the prisoner was hauled off the stage by the guards and shoved onto the back of an open truck lined with two rows of soldiers armed with loaded rifles—always a grim and chilling sight. The truck would set off for the beach, where the executions took place, with hundreds of locals streaming along behind, some on bicycles, some on foot, all flooding toward the shore in a dense black horde. During my childhood years I don't know how many prisoners I saw who crumpled at the knees when they heard their death sentence and had to be dragged forcibly onto the truck.

Once I witnessed this from just a few feet away. The prisoner's hands, tied behind his back, were a ghastly sight, because the cord had been tied so tightly and for such a long time that it had cut off the circulation. His hands had not turned white, as one might imagine they would, but dark purple, almost black. Only later, when I picked up some medical knowledge in the course of my dental training, did I realize that flesh so discolored is damaged beyond recovery. Before this man was shot, his hands were already dead.

We children couldn't possibly run fast enough to keep up with the truck, so often we would try to make an educated guess about which direction it would take, reasoning that if last time the executions were conducted at North Beach, then this time there was a good chance they would be at South Beach. As soon as the rally started we would make a dash for the shore, so that we could stake our claim to plum positions. But sometimes we would arrive at South Beach to find there was absolutely no one there and realized we had run to the wrong place; by then we had no chance of making it to North Beach in time.

On a few occasions we guessed right and so got a grandstand view of the executions. This was the most shocking sight in all my childhood. Armed soldiers formed a semicircle to prevent the spectators from coming too close. The soldier designated to perform the execution would kick the prisoner in the back of the legs, making him drop to his knees. The soldier would take a few steps back, to stay outside the range of blood spray. Then he would raise his rifle, take aim at the back of the prisoner's head, and fire. I was struck by how such a small bullet had such enormous force—more than that of a large shovel—for it would knock the prisoner down to the ground in a second. After that first shot the executioner would go forward to confirm that the prisoner was dead; if still alive, he would need a second bullet. When the soldier turned the body faceup, I would see something that made me shake all over: the entry wound was just a little hole, but where the bullet came out the other side the prisoner's face was shattered beyond recognition, and what had been a forehead was now a gaping crater, as big as the bowl out of which I ate my meals.

Now I need to return to that long and terrifying dream, the nightmare in which I experienced my own destruction. It happened late one night in the final weeks of 1989. I dreamt I was trussed up with cord, a board over my chest, standing at the front of the stage in the high school playing field, two armed guards behind me, landlords, rightists, and counterrevolutionaries arrayed as understudies in the wings, although the "black pen" I mentioned earlier was curiously absent from their ranks. Below the stage was assembled an inky cloud of people whose voices clattered like rain on a sidewalk. Through the loudspeaker I heard a solemn, censorious voice denouncing my various crimes, for it seemed I had committed multiple murders, of varying degrees of depravity. Finally there came the words: **"Sentenced to death, execution immediate."**

No sooner was the sentence read than the soldier behind me took a step forward, slowly raised his rifle, and pointed it at my head. He was standing so close, the muzzle butted my temple. Then I heard a loud bang as he pressed the trigger. The impact of the bullet knocked me off my feet but, strangely, I was somehow able to stand up again and even heard a buzz of noise from below the stage. My head had been split wide open, like an egg that's been cracked, spilling both the white and the yolk. With my empty eggshell of a head I wheeled around to face the executioner and gave a roar of rage. "Hell, we're not at the beach yet!" I cried.

Then I woke, drenched in sweat and heart pounding as always. But now, unlike the earlier occasions, I did not rejoice at the passing of the nightmare, for recovered memories began to torment me. The high school playing field, the sentencing rally, the hands that died ahead of time, the truck and the soldiers armed to the teeth, the shootings on the beach, the bullet so much stronger than a shovel, the little hole at the back of the skull and the gaping cavity in the forehead, the blood slick on the sand—these awful sights replayed themselves endlessly in front of my eyes.

I began to search my conscience: why was I always dreaming at night of being hunted down and killed? Surely it was the result of my writing so much about violence and bloodletting during the day. A karmic law of cause and effect was at work, I became convinced. And so in the hollow of the night—the early hours of the morning, perhaps—under my quilt damp with cold sweat I issued myself a dire warning: You've got to stop writing this kind of story.

Since then twenty years have passed, but when I look back, I still feel a pang of fear. I had pushed myself to the edge of a mental breakdown, and if I had not experienced that particular nightmare and recovered those lost memories, I might have continued to wallow in blood and gore until I'd reached the point of no return. If that had happened, then I would not now be sitting in my home in Beijing, rationally writing these words; instead I might well be slumped in some ramshackle psychiatric hospital, gazing blankly into space.

Sometimes life and writing can actually be very simple: a dream can trigger memory's recall, and everything changes.

鲁迅

lu xun

One day in May 2006 I was sitting in the departure lounge of Copenhagen's well-run airport, surrounded by travelers of multiple nationalities murmuring away in their various languages. I gazed out through the plate-glass windows at the Norwegian Air jet that would soon fly me to Oslo, and my eyes were drawn to the huge portrait on its tail. Whose portrait is that? I wondered. No immediate answer presented itself, and the tantalizing question kept me rooted to my seat. The face looked strangely familiar, with rather long, tousled hair and a pair of old-fashioned spectacles perched on the bridge of his nose.

As boarding began I rose and joined the line at the gate, and soon I had claimed my window seat, still puzzling over the identity of the man on the tail. Just as the plane lifted off from the runway I suddenly realized who he was, for I had seen the very same picture inside a Chinese edition of *Peer Gynt:* it was Henrik Ibsen. Watching Copenhagen gradually slip away behind me, I couldn't help but smile. The world has seen any number of great writers, I thought to myself, but Ibsen must be the most frequent flier among them.

I landed in Oslo one hundred years after Ibsen's death.

The streets were shrouded in a gentle drizzle, and banners imprinted with that same portrait fluttered on both sides of the road, creating two columns of identical portraits—countless Ibsens, near and far, gazing at me in the rain from behind their round spectacles, as though they had a message to impart.

My first meal in Oslo was in a restaurant that Ibsen had often patronized. It had that patina of age one encounters so often in Europe, with round pillars and an exquisite fresco on the high ceiling. To mark the centennial a small round table had been set out near the door; on it lay a black top hat and a just-drained glass of beer, foam still lining its lip. A walking stick stood propped against a vacant chair, suggesting that Ibsen had just stepped away from his table and might return to his seat at any moment.

In the days that followed I did not enter the restaurant again, but I would often pass it as I set off for an engagement or returned late at night. Each time I would pause to take stock of the montage inside and discovered that a subtle change took place during the course of the day: in the morning the glass would be full, but by the evening it would be empty, with that circle of foam around the lip. My curiosity about Ibsen's world made me wonder if he would have been equally curious about mine—if his phantom at the restaurant table might notice a Chinese author coming and going and wonder, "What has this man written?"

It made me think of our own Lu Xun, for it was he who introduced Ibsen's name to Chinese readers in essays written in classical Chinese and published in the monthly periodical *Henan* in 1908, just two years after Ibsen's death. Later, in 1923, Lu Xun would give his famous lecture at Peking Women's College of Education, prompted by Ibsen's play *A Doll's House,* in which he considers what kind of future faces its heroine, Nora Helmer, when she leaves her husband and strikes out on her own. "What happens after Nora leaves?" Lu Xun asked. "Ibsen sheds no light on this—and since he is dead, we cannot ask him. Even if he were still alive, he would not owe us any answers." As a reader of *A Doll's House* Lu Xun then answered the question himself: after Nora leaves, "she has only two real choices: she can either descend into prostitution or she can return to her husband—the only other option being to die of hunger." In Lu Xun's view, for women to deliver themselves from submission and dependency, they needed to gain economic equality with men. Lu Xun continued with typical acerbity:

> Money is an unseemly topic that may well be deplored by gentlemen of lofty principle. But I tend to think that people's views differ not only between one day and the next but also before and after meals. When people admit that money is necessary to feed oneself but still insist on its vulgarity, then one can safely predict that they still have some undigested fish or meat in their systems. They'd sing a different tune, I'm sure, if you made them go hungry for a day.

The portrait of Ibsen on the tail of the plane and its reappearance fluttering on the banners in Oslo streets made me conscious of Ibsen's special status in Norway. He obviously enjoys an exalted reputation in many places, but I have a vague sense that in Norway "Ibsen" does not simply signify the author of classic works but is freighted with a meaning that goes well beyond the scope of literature and biography. In this respect it is similar to the "Lu Xun" of my childhood—that is to say the "Lu Xun" of the Cultural Revolution years. With this thought in mind, when I gave my lecture at the University of Oslo, I told some stories about Lu Xun and me.

The Cultural Revolution was an era without literature, and it was only in our Chinese textbooks that one could catch a faint whiff of literary art. But the assigned texts were confined to the works of just two authors: Lu Xun's stories and essays and Mao Zedong's poetry. In my first year of primary school I believed innocently that there was only one prose author in the world, Lu Xun, and only one poet, Mao Zedong.

In his own day there was surely no author with more highly developed critical instincts than Lu Xun. When the Communist Party came to power in 1949, it claimed that a new society had been inaugurated and in the same breath demanded that the old society be relentlessly condemned. Thus it was that Lu Xun's scathing works were wielded as whips to lash and scourge the supine form of China's past. From an early age we were taught that the despicable old society was "cannibalistic," and Lu Xun's first short story, "Diary of a Madman," was presented as Exhibit A: a fictional story that recorded a madman's ravings about "eating people" was interpreted, to suit the political agenda of the time, as a true statement of social realities. The other stories by Lu Xun adopted as compulsory schoolroom texts—"Kong Yiji," "New Year's Sacrifice," "Medicine," and so on—were likewise read purely as models of how to go about exposing the evils of the old society.

Of course, Mao Zedong's high regard for Lu Xun was a key factor in all this, enabling the writer to enjoy a stellar reputation in the new society, hailed as a threefold great: great author, great thinker, and great revolutionary. Lu Xun died in 1936, but his influence reached its apogee during the Cultural Revolution (which began in 1966) when it was second only to that of Mao himself. In those days almost every essay—whether printed in the newspaper or read out in a radio broadcast or handwritten on a street-side big-character poster—would always, after its obligatory quotations of Mao Zedong, cite some assertion by Lu Xun. Denunciations issued in the name of the people would borrow lines from Lu Xun. The confessions of landlords, rich peasants, counterrevolutionaries, bad elements, and rightists would borrow lines from him, too. "Chairman Mao teaches us" and "Mr. Lu Xun says" were the standard political tags punctuating speeches and articles throughout the land.

There was something paradoxical about the use of that prefix "Mr.," for during the Cultural Revolution this form of address was thoroughly debunked as a Bad Thing associated with feudalism and the bourgeoisie. Lu Xun alone was permitted to enjoy this feudal/bourgeois title, others being known simply as Comrade or, failing that, Class Enemy.

Lu Xun at this time was no longer a controversial author; the intense attacks of which he had once been the target were now a thing of the past. Like the sky washed clean after a storm, this new "Lu Xun" was fresh and radiant. "Lu Xun" had changed from an author to a catchphrase, one that represented eternal correctness and permanent revolution. For a full ten years from primary school through high school, in one textbook after another I glumly read and rehashed the writings of Lu Xun but never could make much sense out of them; I felt only that they were dark, depressing, and utterly tedious. Apart from the occasions when I was putting together a passage of revolutionary invective, where I found it necessary to quote him, the rest of the time his work was basically incomprehensible to me. As a catchphrase, in other words, Lu Xun had his uses, but as a writer I found him a deadly bore. For this reason Lu Xun's writings do not figure at all in my childhood experiences, only Lu Xun the catchphrase.

During my Cultural Revolution years I made the most of this powerful "Lu Xun" phrase. My experience of growing up consisted largely of revolution and poverty, with a good deal of endless argument thrown in. For me argument was a luxury that provided mental nourishment in a life of deprivation.

One argument pitted me against a primary school classmate, the question at issue being: when is the sun closest to the earth? Early morning and late afternoon, he said, for that's when the sun looks biggest. Midday, I said, for that's when the sun is hottest. The two of us began to engage tirelessly in a marathon debate: every day no sooner would we meet than we would reiterate our hypotheses and reject each other's views. After talking this kind of nonsense for goodness knows how long, we began to seek support in other quarters. He took me off to see his sister, who listened to our competing theories and immediately sided with her little brother. Still a couple of years short of puberty, she did not even bother to interrupt the game she was playing. "First thing in the morning and last thing in the afternoon," she said, kicking her shuttlecock. "Of course that's when the sun is closest."

I was not about to throw in the towel and insisted we go and consult my brother. He was naturally just as determined to stand up for his sibling and did so in no uncertain terms. "You better watch yourself," he said, waving both fists in my classmate's face. "If I hear you say morning and afternoon one more time, you're going to get a taste of these."

I found Hua Xu's response disappointing, for I wanted to be vindicated by truth, not by brute force. Off we went in search of slightly older children. Some supported the other boy, some agreed with me; the argument raged back and forth with no clear winner. By the time this had gone on for a year or so, the older children had all served as umpires to our quarrel at one time or another, and they were getting tired of it. Just the sight of us approaching them bickering would make them yell, "Get lost!"

The scope of this acrimonious debate thus confined itself

ultimately to two participants only: him and me. Later my
classmate's views underwent further refinement, and he
found more reasons to cast doubt on my "heat theory": if
temperature is the decisive criterion, he said, does that
mean the sun is closer to earth in the summer and farther
away in the winter? I countered by questioning his "observation theory": if visually confirmed size is what counts,
then does this mean that on a rainy day the sun has got so
small as to completely disappear?

We continued to squabble until the day that I brought
in Lu Xun as my ally; that brought him to his knees soon
enough. In desperation, I had resorted to bluff. "Mr. Lu
Xun has said it, at midday the sun is closest to the earth!"

He looked at me dumbly. "Did Mr. Lu Xun really say
that?"

"Of course he did." I spoke with great assurance, to mask
my guilty conscience. "Don't tell me you don't believe Mr.
Lu Xun?"

"No, it's not that." He waved his hand in alarm. "But why
didn't you say so earlier?"

In for a penny, in for a pound, I thought, as I improvised
madly. "I didn't know before. I just heard it on the radio this
morning."

He hung his head. "If Mr. Lu Xun says this too, it has to
mean you're right and I'm wrong."

It was as simple as that: his position on the distance
between the sun and the earth, which he had defended to
the hilt for twelve months flat, collapsed in ruins at once
before my fictitious Lu Xun. In the days that followed he
was pensive and subdued, tasting alone the bitter flavor of
defeat.

That was a characteristic of the Cultural Revolution era:
no matter whether it was an argument between rebels or
between Red Guards or simply a row between housewives,
the final victor would always come out with something Mao

Zedong had said, so as to crush their opponent and bring the argument to an end. I had originally intended to make up a quotation by Mao but couldn't quite bring myself to utter such an outrageous lie, and so I ended up by changing "Chairman Mao teaches us" to "Mr. Lu Xun says." This way, if my fiction was ever exposed and I was denounced as a little counterrevolutionary, I would at least be charged with a slightly less heinous crime.

As we entered middle school this classmate and I embarked on a new argument, one that would become equally prolonged. This time we found ourselves at odds on the nuclear issue. If one tied all the atomic bombs in the world together and detonated them all at once, he said, the resulting explosion would shatter the earth into a thousand pieces. I disagreed profoundly. The earth's surface, I conceded, would suffer terrible devastation, but the planet itself would suffer no structural damage and would continue to spin on its axis and orbit the sun as it always had.

Discussion evolved into argument, and argument escalated and expanded. In school, throughout the day, we debated for all we were worth, and like election candidates canvassing for votes we each went off to talk others around. Some supported him and some supported me, and the boys in our year were soon divided into two camps: the Earth Destruction School and the Earth Survival School. As time went on everyone else got tired of the argument, leaving just the two of us to carry the torch. Our classmates would shake their heads in despair, and our two competing earths became a standing joke.

One day our argument resumed in the middle of a game of basketball. By this time we had been arguing for months and both felt a need to wrap it up, so there on the court we agreed to consult the chemistry teacher and accept her judgment as the final authority. Off we went, still arguing so contentiously that my companion forgot he was holding

the basketball under his arm. "Hey, hey!" the other boys
cried. "Forget about your two earths, just give us the ball
back!"

The chemistry teacher was a new arrival at the school, a
woman in her thirties who came to us from a city in north
China. We thought her very exotic because she spoke perfect standard Mandarin, unlike the other teachers, who in
class or out spoke only the local dialect. We tracked her
down in the staff room, and after patiently listening to both
points of view, she announced her verdict. "The peoples of
the world are all peace loving," she told us. "How could they
ever think of tying atomic bombs together and detonating
them all at once?"

It had never crossed our minds that the chemistry teacher
would cut the ground out from under us and put such a
damper on our long-standing argument. We retreated from
the staff room in disarray, exchanging discomfited looks and
then unceremoniously dismissing her opinion. "To hell with
her!" we cursed.

We returned to our argument, as obstinate and determined as ever. Forced to desperate remedies once more, I
repeated my earlier ploy. "Mr. Lu Xun has said, even were
one to tie all the atom bombs in the world together and
detonate them, it would not destroy the earth."

"Mr. Lu Xun said that, too?" He eyed me suspiciously.

"You don't believe me?" I decided to brazen it out. "Do
you really think I would make up something Mr. Lu Xun
said?"

My unflinching confidence put him on the defensive.
"No, you wouldn't dare do that," he said, shaking his head.
"Nobody would ever dare make up something Mr. Lu Xun
said."

"Of course not," I said, suddenly stricken with misgiving.

He nodded. "That 'even were one to' sounds a lot like Mr.
Lu Xun."

"What do you mean, 'sounds a lot like'?" I retorted, now flushed with victory. "Those are Mr. Lu Xun's words exactly."

My classmate slunk off to lick his wounds, confounded by his unfortunate tendency to always get on the wrong side of Mr. Lu Xun. A few months later, however, I had quite a scare when I realized what a glaring anachronism I had committed—Lu Xun having died almost ten years before the first atomic bomb was dropped. After several days of anxiety I decided that preemptive action was required. "Last time I misquoted Mr. Lu Xun," I told my classmate. "What he was talking about was bombs, not atomic bombs. What he actually said was: 'Even were one to tie all the bombs in the world together. . . .' "

The boy's eyes lit up. "Bombs and atomic bombs are not the same thing at all!" he said, elated.

"Yes, I can see that." Given the necessity to discourage further inquiries, I had no choice but to acknowledge that I was wrong. "I think you're right. If all the atomic bombs in the world were tied together and detonated, the earth surely would be blown to smithereens."

Our two marathon arguments thus resulted finally in a 1–1 tie. That, of course, is a matter of little consequence, just as the arguments themselves are of no great interest. The real point that emerges here is what absolute authority the phrase "Lu Xun" enjoyed during the Cultural Revolution era.

The story of Lu Xun and me continued to unfold, and in the following episode only he and I were involved. I have gone through some wild passages in my life, and in one of them I put Lu Xun's short story "A Madman's Diary" to music.

I was then in my second year of middle school, which would make it 1974, when the Cultural Revolution had entered its final stages and life continued in its straitjacket

as everyone's apathy deepened. I would play basketball during math class and stroll about on the playground during
chemistry or physics, and there was nothing to stop me.
But after getting sick of the classroom, I got fed up with
the playground, too. I would scowl with frustration at the
length of each day. Freedom was simply tiresome, for there
was nothing I could do with it. It was at this point I discovered music or, to be more precise, I discovered numbered
musical notation, and so in a music class that was just as
boring as math I found renewed pleasure in life. As passion
returned I began to write music.

It was not music itself, I should point out, that enchanted
me, but its numerical notation. I'm not sure why that
was—perhaps it was simply that I knew absolutely nothing
about notation. It was quite different from those Chinese
or mathematics textbooks I leafed through, which I understood if I could be bothered to try. Musical notation, on the
other hand, was a complete mystery to me. All I knew was
that this was how those familiar revolutionary songs presented themselves in print, spilling across the paper like a
bizarre cipher, dimly relating a story in sound. Ignorance
engendered mystery, and mystery became allure, triggering
my creative instincts.

Learning the system of numerical notation was not part
of my plan. Rather, I began my musical composition—the
only music I will ever write in my life, I'm sure—simply
utilizing the outward trappings of that system, taking as
my theme Lu Xun's "A Madman's Diary." First of all I copied Lu Xun's story onto a new homework notebook; then I
inserted notational symbols underneath the text just as the
mood took me. I must have written practically the longest
song tune in the world, a tune that nobody could perform
and nobody would ever be able to hear.

I expended a great deal of energy on this project over a
period of many days, filling up every last line of my notebook

and quite wearing myself out in the process. Throughout I remained in total ignorance of the principles underlying numbered notation. Although I was now in possession of a brand-new opus that took up a whole notebook, I had not advanced one step closer to music and had not the slightest idea what kind of sound my score would produce. I simply felt that it looked a lot like a song, and that in itself was a great source of satisfaction.

I will always have a soft spot for that long-lost composition book and its world's-longest song. My random notation recorded notes higgledy-piggledy, in a meter that was equally chaotic; but it also recorded my existential predicament in the final stages of the Cultural Revolution, a life made up of equal parts stifled instincts, dreary freedom, and hollow verbiage. What made me settle on "A Madman's Diary"? I have no idea. All I know is, after I had written its score, I was unable to find any other literary materials that lent themselves to musical accompaniment and had no choice but to turn my attention to other genres: mathematical equations and chemical reactions. In the days that followed I filled up another composition book with the scores I wrote for them—equally arbitrary meters and haphazard notes, which, if ever performed, would surely make a noise this world has never heard. In hell, I grant you, such sounds may well be part of the ambience, and when I tried to imagine the music I had produced, I tended to hear only the shrieking of ghosts and the howling of wolves. But now and then I would entertain another possibility: that, like a blind cat stumbling on a dead mouse, I had actually struck it lucky, that by some amazing fluke I had written music fit for heaven's ears.

In retrospect, perhaps it's not so strange that I chose "A Madman's Diary" for my compositional experiment, for that title is an apt description of my approach to recording a tune.

After the Cultural Revolution I found it curious that Mao Zedong had held Lu Xun in such high esteem. It was as though these two men were connected psychologically by a secret passageway, for although distance separated them in life and death, they still seemed to maintain a capacity for intercommunication. Both were men of tenacious purpose and restless urges. Mao Zedong praised Lu Xun for his indomitable spirit, but Mao himself had just as firm a backbone, never giving ground in conflicts with the United States and the Soviet Union, although they were stronger than China. And both men, at the deepest level, were fundamental and extreme in their views, vehemently rejecting the Confucian doctrine of the golden mean.

Every great author needs great readers, and for Lu Xun to have such an influential reader as Mao Zedong may have been his good fortune, or it may have been his bad luck. During the Cultural Revolution Lu Xun changed from an author's name to a fashionable political catchphrase, and the man's scintillating and incisive works were submerged under a layer of dogmatic readings. In that era people constantly had "Mr. Lu Xun says" on their lips, in such a familiar tone that you might have thought all Chinese were distantly related to Lu Xun, but very few of them understood him as Mao had. And so, although Lu Xun's reputation reached its pinnacle during the Cultural Revolution, true readers of his work were few and far between. "Mr. Lu Xun says" was really just a way of jumping on the bandwagon.

After the Cultural Revolution Lu Xun was no longer a sacrosanct term in our vocabulary—he reverted to being an author and returned to controversy. Many continued to honor Lu Xun, but there was no shortage of people who took to bad-mouthing him. Such attacks took a different form from those Lu Xun had faced during his own lifetime, now adding sensational elements to the mix as some showed an avid interest in Lu Xun's personal affairs: the four women in his life, his poor showing in bed, his abnormal sexual psychology. . . .

With the rise of China's market-based economy Lu Xun's commercial value keeps being exploited constantly. The characters and places in his stories have been put to work as names for snack foods and alcoholic beverages and tourist destinations; they serve to designate private rooms in night-clubs and karaoke joints, where officials and businessmen, their arms wrapped around young hostesses, sing and dance to their hearts' content.

Some people directly employ Lu Xun as a cheerleader for their products. In the city of Wuhan, for example, a shop specializing in the popular delicacy known as stinky bean curd features Lu Xun in its advertising. The sign at its entrance reproduces a classic photograph of Lu Xun smok-ing, the difference being that the cigarette in his mouth has been digitally erased and replaced with a skewer of stinky bean curd. The proprietor of the shop declares proudly that he and his staff all hail from Lu Xun's hometown of Shao-xing and explains his advertisement as standard practice in China today, drumming up business by exploiting the buzz surrounding celebrity.

The fate of Lu Xun in China—going from being an author to being a catchphrase and then back again—reflects the fate of China itself, and in Lu Xun we can trace the zigzags of history and detect the imprints of our social upheavals.

At the university in Oslo my stories were not quite over. For a time, I told my audience, I was firmly convinced that Lu Xun was a terribly overrated writer whose awesome reputation was nothing more than a by-product of Chinese politics.

In 1984 I was working in the cultural center of a southern

town and beginning to write my own stories. In the hallway outside my office stood a large table, under which were stacked works by Marx, Engels, Lenin, Stalin, Mao Zedong, and Lu Xun. With the passage of time these once-sacred texts had ended up piled in heaps like wastepaper and coated with a thick layer of dust. Lu Xun's books were in the outermost stack, and I would often stub my toes on them as I went in and out of the office. Glancing down at the dusty gray volumes on the floor, I couldn't help but rejoice at their misfortune, thinking to myself, "That guy's days are over, thank goodness!" On one occasion I stumbled over the books and almost landed flat on my face. "Damn it!" I cried. "You're finished, man, but still you try to give me a hard time!"

As the Cultural Revolution ended I had just graduated from high school. In the years that followed I read huge numbers of books but not one word of Lu Xun. When I myself became an author, Chinese critics expressed the view that I was an inheritor of the Lu Xun spirit, a label I found irksome, for I took it as a put-down.

In 1996 I was given an opportunity to reread Lu Xun. A film director was planning to make a movie based on some of his stories and asked me for some ideas on how to approach the adaptation, for a generous fee. Being short of cash at the time, I promptly agreed. Then I realized I didn't have any of Lu Xun's works on my shelves, so I went to a bookstore and purchased a copy of his collected short fiction.

That evening I turned on my desk light and began to read these tales that had so frequently been my required reading and from which I had always felt so estranged. The first story was that same "A Madman's Diary" that I had put to music in my teenage years. Since then I had completely forgotten the plot, and now I reread the story with a fresh eye.

Early on, when the madman senses that the whole world is acting abnormally, he makes the following remark: "Otherwise, why would the Zhaos' dog look at me that way?"

This gave me quite a shock. This Lu Xun fellow knew a thing or two, I thought to myself, to be able to capture a man's lurch into insanity in just one sentence. Other, less talented authors sometimes want a character to lose his senses, but even after they have lavished thirty or forty pages on charting this development, their character still comes across as perfectly sane.

"Kong Yiji" was the third story I read that night. It had appeared over and over again in my Chinese textbooks, but it was not until I was thirty-six years old that I really understood what it was saying. As soon as I finished it, I phoned the director and told him I hoped he would give up on the idea of adapting the stories for the screen. "Don't spoil things," I told him. "Lu Xun doesn't deserve that."

The following day I went to the bookstore and bought a set of *Complete Works of Lu Xun*, in the new edition published after the Cultural Revolution. It made me think back to those books of his under the table in the cultural center, and it seemed to me now that they had been trying to tell me something. When they tripped me up as I went in and out of my office, they were actually dropping a hint, quietly but insistently signaling the presence of a powerful voice within the dusty tomes.

In the month that followed I immersed myself in Lu Xun's lucid and supple writing. "When confronting reality," I would later write, "his narrative moves with such momentum it's like a bullet that penetrates the flesh and goes out the other side, an unstoppable force."

Let me say something more about the story of Kong Yiji. Its opening, though simple, has profound implications. Lu Xun starts by describing the layout of the taverns in Luzhen: how the poor customers in their workingmen's outfits drink standing up, while the affluent customers in their long gowns sit down at a table in the restaurant proper, eating and drinking in comfort. Kong Yiji is the only man in a long gown who stands at the bar. Lu Xun's terse opening announces at the start his character's anomalous social status.

What's particularly notable in the story is that Lu Xun initially makes no mention of how Kong Yiji arrives at the tavern; it is only after his legs are broken in a ferocious beating that the point is addressed. This reflects a great writer's sense of priorities: when Kong Yiji still retains use of both legs, his means of getting around can be left unspecified, but after his legs are broken, the issue becomes paramount. And so we come to the following passage:

> Suddenly I heard a voice: "Give me a warm bowl of wine." The voice was very faint, but it sounded familiar. At first I could not see anyone, but when I stood up and looked more carefully, I found Kong Yiji sitting on the floor, facing the door, his back propped against the counter.

We see him only after we hear him—that in itself is striking. But after "Warming up the wine, I carried the bowl over and set it down on the doorsill" and Kong Yiji pulls out his four coppers in payment, a masterly description follows, in the form of one short sentence: "I saw that his hands were stained with mud and realized he had used them to crawl his way here."

That evening, for me Lu Xun finally changed from a catchphrase to a writer. Looking back on my schooldays, when I was force-fed Lu Xun, I have a variety of reactions: I feel that Lu Xun is not for children at all but for mature, sensitive readers. At the same time I feel that for a reader to truly encounter an author sometimes depends on finding the right moment.

After the Cultural Revolution ended, I read many books—some great, some indifferent. If I ever got tired of a book, I would simply put it aside so that I didn't develop a distaste for its author. But during the Cultural Revolution it was impossible to set Lu Xun's work aside, for I was forced to read him again and again; the result is that Lu Xun is the only author I have ever in my life disliked. When a writer is reduced to a catchphrase, he is bound to be the worse for it.

It did not come as a complete surprise, then, when a Norwegian historian came up to me after my talk and said, "I used to dislike Ibsen in just the same way."

革命

revolution

Some Western intellectuals take the view that an economy can enjoy rapid growth only in a society where the political system is fully democratic. They find it astonishing that in a nation where politics is far from transparent the economy can develop at such an impressive pace. But they are overlooking, I think, a crucial point: behind China's economic miracle there is a pair of powerful hands pushing things along, and their owner's name is Revolution.*

After 1949, when the Communist Party came to power, it steadily maintained its commitment to carry out revolution to the fullest. At that point, of course, revolution no longer meant armed struggle so much as a series of political movements, each hot on the heels of the one before, reaching ultimate extremes during the Great Leap Forward and the Cultural Revolution. Later, when China reintroduced itself to the world in the guise of a freewheeling, market-driven economy, revolution appeared to have vanished. But in our economic miracle since 1978, revolution never disappeared but simply donned a different costume. To put it another way, within China's success story one can see both revo-

°*geming*

lutionary movements reminiscent of the Great Leap Forward and revolutionary violence that recalls the Cultural Revolution.

Let me say something first about the echoes of the Great Leap Forward, starting with some statistics showing the rapid growth of steel output in China. In 1978, the first year of the reforms, it was just over 30 million tons. Two years later, in 1980, it reached 37.12 million tons, the fifth largest steel output in the world. By 1996 it had jumped to No. 1 in the world, where it has stayed ever since. In 2008 it exceeded 500 million tons, or 32 percent of the world's total steel output, more than that of the next seven nations in the world combined. In 2009 China's steel output reached 600 million tons, outstripping by 30 percent the goal set by the government of 460 million tons.

On the positive side, these figures reflect the rapid pace of China's economic growth, but behind them another story is hidden. In 2008 the country's steel capacity reached 660 million tons, of which 460 million tons were consumed in construction and manufacturing, leaving an excess capacity of 200 million tons. One fact about China's steel industry over the past thirty years cannot be glossed over: the speed of the growth in output has clearly outstripped the expansion of the economy. The same kind of frenzied steel production that we saw during the Great Leap Forward has taken place once more on Chinese soil.

During the Great Leap Forward of 1958, under the slogan "Surpass the UK, catch up with the USA," the Chinese people were mobilized to smelt steel. Backyard furnaces filled courtyards in Chinese cities and towns and dotted the Chinese countryside; fires burned everywhere, and smoke billowed across the Chinese sky. Peasants abandoned agriculture for ore extraction and steel production while crops ripened and rotted in the fields. Those employed in the urban sector—workers in pharmaceutical plants and textile mills, department store clerks and cashiers, teachers and students, doctors and nurses—put aside their regular jobs and went off to smelt steel. In that era people were anxious not to be labeled "passive resisters of the Great Leap Forward"; participation in the steel drive was the only route to glory. You can't make steel without ore, so the country people smashed their woks and city people tore down the metal window frames and duct pipes from their work units and homes and tossed them into the backyard furnaces—with results you can imagine. That year China's total steel output was 10.7 million tons, twice the figure of 1957, but at least a third of it was useless scrap. People carried on regardless, smelting steel as the raging fires turned the sky red. They toiled in front of blazing furnaces, sweat streaming down their backs, and as they worked they recited a jingle that captured the spirit of the time, "Let's Compare":

> *You're all heroes and we're all champs,*
> *By the furnace here let's compare our stats.*
> *Good for you, you've smelted a ton—*
> *But a ton and a half is what we've done!*
> *Right, you go off and fly your jet—*
> *Now watch as we launch our rocket!*
> *Your arrow can pierce the sky—*
> *But ours has gone into orbit!*

In the 1990s, as the tide of economic development swept over China, a similar situation began to reappear. In the fields surrounding one large steel plant in eastern China, backyard furnaces went up and in the blink of an eye peasants became sweat-stained steelworkers. After melting the iron ore, they poured it immediately into a specially designed tanker. The driver would stamp his foot on the accelerator and drive the tanker full tilt into the steel plant, where the liquid iron was dumped into a standard industrial furnace for further processing. Under normal circumstances a large furnace produces steel about fourteen times in a twenty-four-hour period, but with the peasants first melting ore in their own furnaces, plants were able to increase production to thirty times a day. Of course, this time what the peasants made in their homegrown furnaces was not useless pig iron, and they were making steel not for some empty political agenda but to put money in their own pockets. Given this frantic effort to make more steel, it's no wonder that China's output has grown so rapidly. Because the tankers carrying liquid iron shuttled back and forth incessantly between the furnaces in the fields and the furnaces in the plants, they discharged so much heat that it roasted road surfaces and converted the leafy trees lining the highways into dry skeletons.

The Great Leap Forward of 1958 began, in a sense, as a comedy—a romantic and absurd comedy. Fakery, exaggeration, and bombast were the order of the day. Even the most productive rice fields at the time could produce only about one and a half tons per acre, but under the slogan "The more boldly a man dares, the more richly his land bears" districts all over the country claimed that per-acre production had topped five tons. On September 18, 1958, for example, the *People's Daily* published a special news report: "Rice production in Huanjiang County, Guangxi, reaches six and a half tons per acre." These bogus reports were fabricated to a high level of detail. Pigs, it was said, now topped the scales at more than eleven hundred pounds; their heads were the size of large wicker baskets, and there was as much meat on them as on three pigs in the old days; a pot three feet tall and three feet wide was not big enough to cook one of these jumbo-sized porkers—why, even with a pot six feet across you could cook only half a pig! Pumpkins had been induced to grow so big that children could play games inside them.

A folk rhyme called "A Sweet Potato Rolling Off the Slope" was all the rage. It went like this:

> *Through our commune fine a stream flows deep,*
> *By the riverside the hill climbs steep.*
> *We pick sweet potatoes on its lee,*
> *Laughing and joking, merry as can be.*
> *Then, a sudden splash—a huge fountain of spray,*
> *"Oh, no!" I cry, and jump up in dismay.*
> *"Who fell in? I hope they can swim!"*
> *Everyone chuckles, thinking me dim:*
> *"Don't worry, no need to throw in a rope—*
> *That was just a sweet potato rolling off the slope!"*

In August 1958 administrative units at the township level were abolished and replaced in one fell swoop with People's Communes. Then, at one more fell swoop, communal dining halls were established: peasants no longer ate in their own homes but went to the dining halls to feast. "Stuff yourselves full, then redouble production" was the slogan of the hour. Communal dining halls consumed grain without any kind of planning and recklessly wasted resources, sometimes promoting eating contests. In their efforts to win the Top Trencherman award peasants were known to get so bloated they had to be carted off to the hospital.

Within a few months grain depots everywhere were empty. The curtain fell on that absurd romantic comedy, and in its place the stage was set for a cruel and all too realistic tragedy. Famine ruthlessly enveloped China. Because regions had falsely reported the size of their harvests, the state's grain procurement was vastly greater than actual output. Local officials had inflated their production figures to impress their superiors, and now it was the peasants who paid the price, for their grain ration, seed grain, and feed grain were all requisitioned by the state. Some localities, in the name of the revolution, began a savage campaign to ferret out those engaged in "concealment of produce and private distribution," and officials in communes and production brigades were ordered to establish "grain-inspection shock teams" that conducted house-by-house searches, turning the occupants' possessions upside down, rooting around in their yards, and searching inside walls. If the teams were unable to find grain to confiscate, they would take it out on the hapless peasants. In one such campaign by Xiaoxihe Commune in Anhui's Fengyang County, more than three thousand people were beaten; of these one hundred suffered crippling injuries and thirty or more perished while undergoing "reform through labor" imposed by the commune. At this point, hunger came roaring in like a hurricane and death tightened its grip on one province after another. According to official figures released later, during the Great Leap Forward, in Sichuan Province alone, more than eight million people died of hunger—one in every nine residents.

Even after so many years, while people still reflect on the disaster of the Great Leap Forward, that same type of development keeps rearing its head in our economic life. One sees signs of it in the frenzy to construct airports, harbors, highways, and other such large-scale public works. These projects in theory must first win approval from the central government, but in reality many local governments first launch their project and only later submit it for approval. Thus impractical, extravagant, and duplicate initiatives are common, and they are pursued as vigorously as a revolutionary campaign. Take port construction as an example. Along the four hundred miles of coast in Hebei and Tianjin there are no fewer than four major ports: Qinhuangdao, Jingtang, Tianjin, and Huanghua. In 2003, although all four ports were underutilized, this did not stop them from constantly increasing investment and expanding their facilities.

With the rapid growth of the Chinese economy, some of the more forward-looking Great Leap Forward–type construction projects have progressed quickly from being undernourished to having indigestion. But other such projects remain in a state of persistent neglect. Some expressways, like the Shi-Huang Highway in Hebei and the Tai-Jing Highway in Jiangxi, have been in service for more than ten years but rarely see more traffic than just a few cars and tour buses. The Internet is rife with jokes about how you could hold a Formula One Grand Prix on one of these highways any day of the week, or that they would be great places to go for a nice quiet honeymoon.

In 1999 the Ministry of Education decided to greatly expand enrollments in higher education, and China's educational Great Leap Forward began. In 2006 institutions of higher education recruited 5.4 million new students, five times as many as in 1998; the total number of those enrolled was 25 million. The ministry proudly declared:

> In the scale of its higher education, China has overtaken Russia, then India, and now the United States, to become No. 1 in the world. In just a few short years of assiduous effort, under conditions where per capita GDP is just US$1,000, higher education in China has achieved the shift from elite to widespread education, completing a process that other countries have needed forty or fifty years—or even longer—to complete.

Behind all the glorious statistics in China today, crises tend to lurk. The loans that Chinese universities have relied on to fund their enrollment expansion already exceed 200 billion yuan. This staggering debt is likely to become another fiasco for China's commercial banks, because Chinese universities lack the wherewithal to repay their loans. At the same time, university tuition in the past ten or fifteen years has risen enormously, to twenty-five or even fifty times as much as it used to be, ten times the rate of income growth. Supporting a college student today is estimated to require the equivalent of 4.2 years of an urban net income or 13.6 years of a rural net income. The Great Leap Forward type of enrollment growth has created immense difficulties in the job market: every year we are adding more than 1 million college graduates who cannot find work. Many low-income parents are prepared to bankrupt themselves and take on enormous debt to put their children through college; but after graduation those children join the army of unemployed, and their parents can only sink deeper into financial hardship. Given this harsh reality, some children are forced to abandon their dreams: as soon as they graduate from high school they put a bedroll on their backs and become migrant laborers instead. In 2009, after thirty-two years of increases, there was actually a drop in the number of high school students taking the university entrance examination.

Let's now consider how the revolutionary violence of the Cultural Revolution has continued to rear its head in the course of China's economic success story of the past thirty years. Here it helps to know something about official seals. Round wooden seals less than two inches in diameter, they weigh no more than a pack of cigarettes, but in our sixty years under communism these insubstantial-looking accessories have often been the concrete emblems of immense political and economic power. Documents of appointment require an official seal, contracts between companies require a seal, and seals also provide verification of whether one possesses legal status: work ID, student ID, birth certificates, death certificates, marriage certificates, and so forth all require authentication with an official seal. In China official seals are needed everywhere, all the time.

In January 1967 the rebel faction in Shanghai launched an

assault on the city government, snatching away the government's official seal and announcing the successful seizure of power. This was the celebrated "January Revolution." Similar movements then convulsed the entire country as rebel factions and Red Guards everywhere launched attacks on their government organs, on factories and schools, and on People's Communes. These nationwide power seizures amounted, in a sense, to a movement to seize official seals. Like robbers or bandits, rebels and Red Guards smashed open the doors and windows of government buildings and factories and schools, rushed in exultantly, and broke into desks and cabinets, ransacking offices in their search for these symbols of authority.

Whoever seized the official seal would be the possessor of true power; they could issue orders right and left and allocate funds with supreme confidence, destroy the lives of people they disliked, and use public money to bankroll their expenses. Any and all actions would be instantly legitimized, so long as they were recorded on a piece of paper and stamped with the official seal.

As a result, deadly struggles developed between different rebel factions and Red Guard organizations, with both sides intent on seizing official seals. Sometimes several organizations would launch simultaneous attacks on government offices, all eager to be first to seize the seal. They would scale walls and jump through windows—whatever it took to get the jump on their rivals. It sometimes looked a lot like a game of American football, for as one group tried to break into the offices, another group would fearlessly hurl themselves at them, tugging on their jackets and wrestling them to the ground so as to enable their comrades to enter the building first. Sometimes a rebel faction had just managed to seize the government seal, only to discover that other rebel organizations already had them surrounded.

I witnessed one such scene myself when I was seven years

old. Standing under a willow tree, I watched, transfixed, as a revolutionary power seizure took place on the other side of the river. A dozen or more rebels had rushed inside the three-story building that housed the local government offices. They had just given a whoop of delight to celebrate their seizure of the seal when a different group of rebels arrived on the scene. There were forty or fifty of them, armed with clubs, and they soon had the offices completely surrounded. Their commander picked up a megaphone and barked out an instruction to the rebels inside, telling them to hand over the seal without further delay. And if they refused? "You may have gone in on your own two legs," he threatened, "but they'll have to bring you out on stretchers."

The defenders had a megaphone of their own. "You've got to be joking!" they fired back. They followed this with a chorus of "Long Live Chairman Mao!"

The besiegers responded with their own "Long Live Chairman Mao!" and charged inside, waving their clubs. Amid cries of "Long Live Chairman Mao!" and "Defend Great Leader Chairman Mao to the Death!" the two groups of combatants clashed in a frantic melee. From my side of the river I could dimly make out the sounds of glass shattering, clubs and chairs breaking, and howls of pain. The occupiers, vastly outnumbered, were forced to give ground, finally evacuating to the flat concrete roof. Two of their wounded had to be dragged up the stairs; they lay motionless on the roof, just barely alive. Soon the other rebels launched their final assault, clubs flailing, and three of the defenders were knocked right off the roof. One of them was clutching the seal in his hand, and just before he fell he threw it as far as he could into the river below.

The attackers had won the battle, only to see their most valuable prize now floating off downstream. They rushed out of the building, yelling wildly. One of the rebels raced ahead to a wooden bridge; there he stripped off his clothes and slipped out of his cotton shoes, then threw himself into the chilly waters. Amid the cheers of his comrades on the bank, he splashed his way into the middle of the current and grabbed the seal before it sank below the surface.

Afterward the town's new power holders conducted a victory parade. The intrepid swimmer, still soaking wet, led the way, clutching the seal in his right hand. His comrades followed close behind, some with blood on their faces, others hobbling along, living proof of how fierce the fighting had been. In between yells of "Long Live Chairman Mao!" they announced that the "January Revolution" in our town had now achieved total victory. The man who had risked his life to recover the seal was now a local hero. In the days that followed, more than once I saw him come to an abrupt stop as he walked down the street, give an enormous sneeze, then continue on his way.

Chinese society now is radically different from what it was during the Cultural Revolution, but the status of official seals has not changed in the slightest: they remain the symbol of political and economic power. So seizures of official seals continue to take place in China today.

Owing to tensions among shareholders, some privately run companies have seen farcical to-and-fro tussles where the company's seal keeps changing hands. Shareholders may look so proper in their suits and leather shoes, but if they want to grab control of the company, they will seize the official seal with as little delicacy as underworld thugs. They punch and kick, spit and curse, smash chairs and break cups, quite indifferent to the impression they give the employees. This kind of episode has also been known to occur in law offices, when lawyers who pride themselves on their legal knowledge vie for possession of the company seal just as fiercely as bandits in the old days competed to abduct women. Even in state-run enterprises, seizures of seals sometimes happen. Such companies are nominally led by a board of trustees, but their traditional party committee structure remains entrenched. In 2007 the party secretary of one state-run enterprise, at loggerheads with the chairman of the board, dismissed him in the name of the party committee—despite the fact that legally only a board of trustees has the power to take such action. Then the party secretary brought in dozens of toughs to smash open the door of the chairman's office with sledgehammers and pry open his cabinet, carrying off the company seal.

Such incidents happen not only internally within enterprises; they often take place between companies, and even between government entities. In one case, for example, a company in south China lost a lawsuit because its rival had produced testimony from a third company that served to discredit it. The defendant appealed the ruling and, before the appeal was heard, fabricated a different document ascribed to this third company, going to extreme lengths to make it appear authentic. Several of the defendant's enforcers pushed their way into the third company's offices—the staff were so intimidated that they hid in a bathroom—and then broke into a filing cabinet, took out the company seal, and stamped the doctored documents. When the case was heard, the defendant proudly brought out the documents in support of its case, rejecting all claims that the documents were fake and the seal was invalid.

In another case, one government agency seized another's seal. Ten acres of land under a village's jurisdiction had been requisitioned by higher authorities in the adjacent city, but the village and the city had not been able to reach agreement on the selling price. The city tried to force the village committee into compliance, but under pressure from rank-and-file villagers the village committee refused to ratify the proposed agreement. The city government, exasperated, sent people into the village to snatch away the seal, then stamped the agreement in the village committee's name.

From the Cultural Revolution to the present, there are countless such examples; sometimes there are striking similarities between things that happened then and things that are happening now. A friend told me that during the power-seizure phase of the Cultural Revolution a factory in the town where he lived had two separate rebel organizations. They were of equal strength, and their commanders understood that they would suffer serious casualties if they were to fight over the seal. So they negotiated a power-sharing agreement: the factory seal would be cut into two, and each faction would retain half. When both commanders agreed on a particular course of action, they would produce their half-seals and press them together on a letter or directive, then pocket them once more. In the stamp on the finished documents a crack could clearly be seen.

Years later, in the reform era, another story of a cracked seal is linked to a private entrepreneur's rise to glory. Today he leads a large enterprise, but to start with he was just the deputy manager of a small company. Like a rebel activist in the Cultural Revolution, he gathered a group of like-minded people around him. First he frightened the manager into vacating his position, and then he threatened to break the legs of the chairman of the board, forcing him out, too. Now he was chairman of the board and manager combined.

The original chairman took the company seal away with him when he fled, and without the seal the company could not conduct normal business. But the new boss man wasn't going to let such a petty detail stand in his way. In Chinese cities you can find tucked away in every neighborhood small businesses that will make you an official seal on the quiet, so he told an underling to go out and get a new seal carved. This was illegal, since official seals require a letter of authorization from the relevant government department, but for a man with entrepreneur's ambitions legal niceties counted for nothing. Having a seal of his own did not entirely resolve the issue, however, because the existence of the other seal could still hamstring the company's operations; the original chairman of the board might use it to sign contracts, for example, sowing all kinds of confusion.

But to the businessman, that was a minor detail, too. When his aide arrived with the newly carved seal, he told him to go out again and buy an axe. The assistant could make no sense of that but did his bidding all the same, then watched in astonishment as his new boss put the seal on his desk, raised the axe, and cleaved the seal neatly in two. Finally, he confirmed his authority with an announcement that, henceforth, contracts approved by the company would need to have a cracked stamp to be genuine; those with an unblemished stamp would be fakes.

Such acts of intimidation are common among some Chinese entrepreneurs, who not only rely on beatings to seize control but will even hire people to kill their rivals, putting the mafiosi in Hollywood movies completely in the shade.

As China's economy has raced forward, violence reminiscent of the Cultural Revolution has taken place not only on the popular level but also with official backing. Just consider how urbanization has been pursued, with huge swathes of old housing razed in no time at all and replaced in short order by high-rise buildings. These large-scale demolitions can make Chinese cities look as though they have been targets of a bombing raid. In a joke once popular among urban residents, the CIA was said to have traced Osama bin Laden to a hideout in their city. A spy plane enters the airspace overhead, only to discover a scene of utter devastation. "I don't know who ordered the bombing," the American pilot reports back to headquarters, "but there's no way bin Laden could have survived this."

Behind the situation is a developmental model saturated with revolutionary violence of the Cultural Revolution type. To suppress popular discontent and resistance, some local governments send in large numbers of police to haul away any residents who refuse to budge. Then a dozen or more giant bulldozers will advance in formation, knocking down a blockful of old houses in no time at all. When the residents are finally released, they find only rubble where their homes once stood. Vagrants now, they have no option but to bow to reality and accept the housing offered.

In a typical case, back in 2007, a family of five was unable to reach agreement with the local authorities on compensation for the loss of their house and found themselves forcibly evicted. One night as they were sleeping, a gang of men in hard hats threw ladders up against the outside wall, smashed the windows with hammers and clubs, and jumped inside. The family woke to find themselves surrounded by dozens of intruders. Before they were fully aware of what was happening, they were dragged from their beds like criminals and rushed downstairs without being allowed to dress or collect any personal effects; any resistance was met with a punch in the jaw. They were shoved into a van and taken off to an empty house. There they sat, huddled in their bedcovers, on a cold concrete floor, guarded by a couple of dozen policemen, until noon that day, when an official came in and informed them that their house had been razed and their property inventoried and moved to a new address. Given the fait accompli, they had no choice but to move into the house assigned them. When they talked about the incident afterward, it seemed more like a scene in a movie than real life, for it had all happened so suddenly. "Even in a war, you give your enemy some time to surrender," they moaned.

Our economic miracle—or should we say, the economic gain in which we so revel—relies to a significant extent on the absolute authority of local governments, for an administrative order on a piece of paper is all that's required to implement drastic change. The method may be simple and crude, but the results in terms of economic development are instantaneous. That is why I say it is the lack of political transparency that has facilitated China's breakneck growth.

Violent evictions are all too common in China today, provoking many acts of collective resistance. In November 2009, in a city in the southwest, dozens of men carrying steel pipes and crowbars burst into the homes of nine families whose houses were earmarked for demolition. The men stuck duct tape over the mouths of some thirteen residents and hustled them into waiting vehicles; four of the homeowners were injured in the struggle. Then two earthmoving machines revved their engines and demolished twenty-six houses within a matter of minutes. Yet more violent confrontation ensued after daybreak, when the outraged evictees and their friends and relatives—some thirty people or more—blocked the nearby intersection with red cotton strips and more than forty liquefied gas canisters, demanding an apology from the local government. On the ground that the roadblock was disrupting the social order, police dispersed them and detained four instigators on charges of fomenting a disturbance and obstructing traffic.

In the same month a woman's house was forcibly demolished by the local government because she refused to sign a resettlement agreement that stipulated compensation at what was obviously below-market value. As the bulldozer knocked open the front door and began to ram the outer walls, and her house began to rupture and collapse, she drank a large glass of whiskey to bolster her courage; then, aided by her husband, she stood on her fourth-floor balcony and tossed Molotov cocktails at the earthmover and the demolition crew, who retaliated by throwing stones at her. Despite her stubborn resistance, after several hours her apartment too was flattened; later the couple was found guilty of obstructing public works and her husband was sentenced to eight months in prison.

Also that same month, on November 11 in Chengdu, a woman named Tang Fuzhen took things one step further. After attacking a demolition crew with Molotov cocktails and putting up resistance for more than three hours, she doused herself with gasoline and ignited it with a cigarette lighter, burning herself to death. This incident finally triggered a furor in the Chinese media, and although the local government classified her self-immolation as violent resistance to the law, public opinion sided with Tang Fuzhen. People began to question the legality of the Regulation Governing House Demolition and Resettlement in Urban Areas, and five professors at Peking University Law School sent a proposal to the Standing Committee of the National People's Congress recommending that the regulation be revised, pointing out that it conflicts with both the Constitution and the Property Rights Law.

In the past few years social contradictions triggered by forced demolitions have become more and more common, and social conflicts have become more intense. Tang Fuzhen's suicide triggered resentments that had long been building up, and in the face of strong public pressure the State Council indicated that it would revise the Regulation Governing House Demolition and Resettlement in Urban Areas. But just as many people were expecting a crackdown on forced demolition and resettlement, reality has exposed their naivety, for such incidents, far from diminishing, have if anything become even more grave.

Late on the night of March 26, 2011, twenty mechanical diggers and several hundred men armed with pickaxes suddenly descended on a residential compound affiliated with Changchun Film Studio in Jilin Province. Fourteen buildings were razed to the ground in a matter of just five hours. Not only were there forcible evictions, but some residents were carried out and dumped like garbage outside their homes. A fifty-year-old woman named Liu Shuxiang, trapped in her room, was crushed under fallen masonry and had died by the time police finally came to investigate, two days later.

There are bizarre cases as well. In one locality, forty-odd state employees found their jobs threatened because their relatives would not agree to demolition and resettlement. A district administrator informed his subordinates that if they failed to persuade their kinfolk, thus delaying relocation, they would all be fired. In the villages where the recalcitrant relatives lived, the public address system reverted to Cultural Revolution routine, continually broadcasting demolition-and-resettlement ultimatums from eight in the morning till six in the evening. "The government is fully committed to this project," the loudspeakers blared. "Nothing will be permitted to stand in its way."

These episodes, old and new, remind me of something Mao Zedong once said. Mao offered a memorable definition of what revolution means, and during the Cultural Revolution we could recite it backward. It went like this:

> A revolution is not a dinner party, or writing an essay,
> or painting a picture, or doing embroidery; it cannot be
> so refined, so leisurely and gentle, so temperate, kind,
> courteous, restrained, and magnanimous. A revolution
> is an insurrection, an act of violence.*

I n the early summer of 1972 several boys slipped quietly out of their classes at Bright Sky Primary School and headed off in the sunshine toward Haiyan Secondary School. To get there, they had to cross a river, by way of a newly con-

---

*Selected Works of Mao Tse-tung, vol. 1 (Peking: Foreign Languages Press, 1965), p. 28.

structed concrete bridge. Workmen had laid straw sacks across the road and were spraying them with rubber hoses to keep the fresh concrete damp and prevent cracks. The wet straw squelched under my feet until I reached the other side—it was my first time playing truant. My classmates and I could hardly contain our curiosity on this walk to the school we would be entering that autumn, for there was one thing we were very eager to find out: what is revolution?

At this point, having experienced six years of Cultural Revolution, we had seen and heard of many revolutionary incidents, but we had never actually taken part. Although we had often parroted that phrase of Mao's "To rebel is justified," this idea had always been confined to the level of speech and had never been put into action. Boys who were a year or two older treated us with condescension. "You don't know shit," they would say. "You lot need to wait till you're in middle school to know what revolution is."

This was a big blow to my self-esteem, because before this I had always assumed that my life was firmly grounded in revolution. For a street urchin like me the experience of growing up consisted of streets full of red flags and big-character posters: I had observed countless demonstrations and acts of violence, and trailing along behind grown-ups, I had gone to watch innumerable struggle meetings.

At that time the people I most admired were boys ten years older than me, for they had been able to participate in the nationwide "networking" by Red Guards that had begun in October 1966. Schools canceled classes so that everyone could take part in revolutionary activities, and Red Guards embarked on ambitious journeys designed to "develop connections" and "exchange experiences." China then was dotted with Red Guard Reception Stations, which arranged room and board, disbursed travel expenses, catered to the young activists' material needs, and lined up transportation to ferry them back and forth. The Red Guards from our town had only small change to their name—a yuan or two at most—but with an officially stamped networking letter of introduction they were able to roam the whole country from east to west and north to south—no need to fork out money for train tickets or hotels or even pay for their meals. No wonder they looked so enraptured later, when they recalled their networking adventures.

One of those roaming Red Guards was the older brother of a classmate of mine. By this time the brother had been relocated to a rural village, where he endured a life of back-breaking toil. Every couple of months he would walk five or six hours to get back to our town, and a few days later walk another five or six hours back to a village where the only nighttime lighting came from kerosene lamps. His home visits were holiday occasions for us younger children, and listening to his stories on those summer evenings was a cherished pleasure.

As the heat receded at the end of the day, he would sit back in a rattan chair, his right foot resting on his left knee and a palm-leaf fan in his hand. Soon a dozen or more admirers would park themselves on the ground in front of him, and he would travel back in time to that morning when he and his comrades had raised their red banners and marched majestically out of our little town, their Red Guard armbands gleaming. They planned to march five hundred miles to Shaoshan, in Hunan, where they would pay homage at Mao Zedong's ancestral home, then march another five hundred miles to Mao's earliest revolution-ary base area, the Jinggang Mountains of Jiangxi. But they wore themselves out just on the first day's march, so instead they flagged a truck down and rode in the back as far as Shanghai, fifty miles away. After touring Shanghai for a good ten days or so, they took a train to Beijing, where they did more sightseeing, and then divided into two groups, one boarding the train to Qingdao, the other traveling south to Wuhan. Over time their numbers dwindled, and in the end my classmate's brother constituted a team of one. He traveled by himself to Guangzhou, where he ran into Red Guards from Shenyang, in the northeast, and in their company crossed the strait to Hainan Island. Six months later, he and his Red Guard associates, like soldiers separated in battle, straggled back to our town one by one. Exchanging notes about their respective networking activities, they realized that not one of them had made it to Shaoshan or the Jinggang Mountains. They had gone only to major cities and famous tourist destinations, and in the name of the revolution had accomplished the longest and most enjoyable sightseeing excursion of their entire lives. The story always ended with a stirring refrain: "Ah, our beautiful rivers and mountains—I saw them all, you know!"

By that time the Red Guard veterans from our town had been banished to the countryside and were living in wretched conditions. After the chaos and turmoil of the early phase of the Cultural Revolution, Mao Zedong was confronted by a harsh reality: for three years after 1966, high schools and universities had admitted no new students, creating a backlog of more than 16 million middle school and high school graduates awaiting further education or employment. Although society had become relatively more stable, China's economy was on the verge of bankruptcy and could offer no new openings for urban employment. Mao's Red Guards had shown their mettle in large-scale fighting and property confiscations and were all too accustomed to beating people, smashing things up, and stealing. Unless they had something to keep them busy, 16 million Red Guards and urban youth were in danger of becoming a destabilizing force in society.

Mao Zedong saw that something needed to be done. "Let educated youth go to the countryside," he said, with a wave of his hand. "There they can receive further education from the poor and lower-middle peasants."

Countless families were affected, and many tragedies ensued. Children said good-bye to their tearful parents and left home with a simple bedroll on their backs, heading off for border regions and rural villages. Transplanted into China's poorest areas, they began a life of deprivation, of sad partings and all too short reunions. Of the high school graduates in our town who "went up to the mountains and down to the villages," some were sent to Heilongjiang, a thousand miles away, and others were relocated to hinterland areas in their home province. These former Red Guards were now pessimistic and despondent about their future prospects. Every time they came home on a few days' furlough, they waxed nostalgic about their networking during the early stages of the Cultural Revolution and loved to regale us with vivid accounts of their adventures. But somehow it was their reports of what happened at the train stations that I remember best.

As they networked, Red Guards crammed into all the trains running on Chinese tracks. Some managed to stretch out underneath the seats, and some squeezed themselves onto the luggage racks overhead, but most had to settle for standing hour after hour as their train wended its way slowly from one stop to the next. The toilets were even more congested than they would be on my train out of Beijing twenty years later, so it was utterly impossible to use the facilities. As soon as the train pulled into a station, the Red Guards would pour out of doors and windows like toothpaste squirting endlessly from a tube; boys would boldly unbuckle their belts and urinate and defecate right there on the platform, while girls would huddle in circles, taking turns to squat down and do their business within this human shield, hidden from the prying gaze of boys with wicked notions. Then the Red Guards, boys and girls alike, would squeeze back into the carriages and the train would pull away, leaving the platform dotted with foul-smelling piles and puddles.

My classmate's older brother was for a time the symbol of revolution in my eyes, because he loved to tell stories about his experiences as a Red Guard traveling the country. Later, however, after a bamboo flute appeared in his hand, he no longer talked about his splendid adventures and instead became silent and subdued. Each time he returned from the countryside, he arrived wearing mud-stained old sneakers, carrying an old canvas duffel bag in his right hand and the flute in his left. It would be much the same picture when he headed back a few days later, except that by then his mother would have washed his shoes. During his time at home he would sit by the window playing his flute—fitful, fragmentary snatches of revolutionary anthems that, as performed by him, lost their impassioned energy and took on a decadent lassitude. Sometimes he would simply sit at the window, a blank look on his face, and if we went up and said hello, he made no effort to acknowledge us.

Once so communicative, he had become a different person, taciturn and glum. Perhaps his flute had replaced speech, giving expression to the complex of emotions that he could never put into words. During those two years, any time I heard the trill of a bamboo flute as I was walking down our lane, I knew that he had come home. The only flute music ever heard in our alley, it served to signal his existence. Now and again he would play the tune of a peddler hawking pear-syrup candy, which would induce us younger kids to come running in his direction, eager for a treat. Seeing our chagrin at having been duped, he would chortle with amusement, then revert to his customary silence.

This erstwhile totem of revolution died during my final year in primary school. He had come back home again and this time stayed for a couple of weeks, refusing to return to the countryside. As I passed his house I would often hear his father cursing him as a slacker and a good-for-nothing. In a feeble voice he would dispute this, saying he simply felt so exhausted he just didn't have the energy to work in the fields. "You're as lazy as a little bourgeois!"—his father's voice went up a notch as he poured scorn on this lame excuse—"Idlers are always complaining they've got no energy."

His mother felt it wouldn't do to keep on arguing like this, nor was it practical for their son to stay on indefinitely, for it would just lead others to conclude that the problem was ideological. She did everything she could to talk him around, and finally he gave in. On the day of his departure she slipped a couple of hard-boiled eggs in his jacket pocket—they were luxury items in those days. I glimpsed him as he left. By then he was as thin as a rake and his complexion had a yellowish tinge. He shuffled off with his head bowed, the flute in his left hand, that battered old duffel bag in his right, his old sneakers on his feet. He was sobbing and kept rubbing his eyes with his left sleeve.

That was the last time I saw him on his own two feet. A few days later, out in the fields, he collapsed on the ground and ended up being carried into the county hospital on a door panel. The doctors diagnosed his condition as late-stage hepatitis and rushed him off to Shanghai, but he died in the ambulance on the way there. According to my father, when they examined him in the hospital, they found that his liver had shrunk to a minuscule size and was as hard as a stone. With his passing, the flute that had graced my childhood forever fell silent.

What is revolution? The answers I have heard take many forms. Revolution fills life with unknowables, and one's fate can take an entirely different course overnight; some people soar high in the blink of an eye, and others just as quickly stumble into the deepest pit. In revolution the social ties that bind one person to another are formed and broken unpredictably, and today's brother-in-arms may become tomorrow's class enemy.

Two scenes linger before my eyes, one that sums up for me the beauty of the human character and another that epitomizes its ugliness.

The first of those images is that of a classmate's father. He became a target of attack when I was in first grade; being just a low-level official in the Communist Party apparatus did not protect him from being labeled a capitalist-roader. I liked him because he recognized me as his son's classmate and always smiled at me in the street—the only grown-up to do so, so far as I can remember. After he became a target, I never saw that heartwarming smile again, and if we ran into each other, he would quickly look away. During his months on the blacklist he must have been subjected to all kinds of mistreatment; every time I saw him, his face was battered and bruised. My classmate, once a cheerful, care-free boy, now had terror in his eyes, and during recess he would stand by himself in a corner as the rest of us played. One morning he arrived at school crying and sobbing, and as he stood waiting for the bell to ring, his whole body shook and he buried his face in his hands. His father, we soon learned, had drowned himself in a well. The culmination of many weeks of suffering, his suicide was surely not an impetuous act on his part, but he had taken great care to conceal his intentions from his loved ones. Torn between staying and leaving, in the end he elected death; in the early hours of the morning he rose silently, bade a sound-less farewell to his sleeping wife and son, then opened the door and took that leap into another world. I had seen him in the street just a few hours before. Blood was trickling down his forehead, and he was walking with a limp. In the failing light of that late afternoon, his right hand rested on his son's scrawny shoulders, and as he talked to the boy, he wore a smile of seeming nonchalance. Many years later, as I wrote *Brothers* at my home in Beijing, I was always haunted by that spectacle of a father walking with his son on the last evening of his life. It was out of that indelible image, perhaps, that Song Fanping emerged to live and die in the pages of my book.*

The ugliness I observed in second grade. As we children ran around during recess, our teachers would stand in the playground in clusters of two or three, exchanging a few words while they kept a watchful eye on us. A couple of the second-grade women teachers would regularly stand next to each other and chatter away jovially. Often I would hear them cackling over some amusing story and I would throw them an envious glance, for it seemed to me they had a special rapport, like sisters who share all their inner thoughts. One morning, however, I arrived at school early, before anybody else had arrived in the playground. I went into the classroom to find one of the teachers already at her desk, correcting homework. Looking up, she beckoned me conspiratorially and told me with unmistakable excitement and relish that her colleague was the daughter of a landlord—something the school had just learned, after sending someone to her hometown to conduct inquiries—and now she was in custody and facing investigation. When I realized how this teacher was savoring the other's downfall, I was struck with horror, for all along I had been so sure they were best friends. Later I would always shudder when I saw teachers in the playground engaged in seemingly intimate conversation. Even the gruesome street battles didn't frighten me as much as that false veneer of camaraderie.

What was revolution? In my early years I had a living

---

*In Yu Hua's most recent novel, *Brothers,* Song Fanping is father and step-father to the main characters, Song Gang and Baldy Li.

example before me, in the shape of my brother. Hua Xu was born, it seemed, for revolutionary agitation; "To rebel is justified" could have been his blood type. When still in second grade, he performed a revolutionary feat that shocked the whole school. His grade teacher had criticized him, in harsh language that he found offensive, for disrupting class. He rose to his feet, picked up his chair, and carried it to the side of the rostrum where the teacher was standing. As she watched in bewilderment, he jumped up on the chair and from this commanding height smashed his fist into the side of her head, just above her ear. Though just nine years old, he managed to deliver a knockout punch; the next thing the teacher knew, she was lying in a hospital bed.

Once he entered middle school, Hua Xu's revolutionary nature found even richer soil to till. The testimony of his language-and-literature teacher left a deep impression on me: when pushed beyond her limits, she took the step of visiting us at home and delivering to my parents a long list of grievances, interspersed with bouts of tears. To catalog all her charges took her quite some time, and one particular episode she recounted has always stayed in my mind.

During class one day that winter, Hua Xu had taken off his sneakers and laid them on the windowsill to dry out in the sun. His nylon socks gave off a rank stench, all the more intrusive because he sat in the front row and put his feet on the top of his desk. As the teacher introduced the lesson, she had altogether too close an encounter with the stink emanating from my brother's direction. She told him to put his shoes on. No, he couldn't do that, he said; his footwear required a further period of exposure to the sun. So saying, he wiggled his toes ostentatiously, the better to distribute his foot odor. Goaded beyond endurance, the teacher stormed over, picked up the shoes, and chucked them out the window. But Hua Xu knew how to counter that: he jumped onto his desk, and from there onto the rostrum, where he grabbed the teacher's notes, then ran over to the window and tossed them out, too. Amid the cheers of his classmates he then jumped out the window and climbed back in again, sneakers in hand. Returning his shoes to their preferred location, he plopped himself down in his chair and put his feet back on his desk. Finally, like a conductor leading an orchestra, he waved his hands in the air to direct his classmates' applause and watched in triumph as the teacher shuffled dejectedly out of the classroom. She could not bring herself to hop out and back in the window as my brother had done, so was forced to make a long detour around the building to retrieve her notes. As she bent down to pick them up off the ground, she noticed her pupils' faces glued to the windows and heard a gloating chorus of mockery.

My father was incensed. No sooner did he see the teacher out the door than he sprang into action, grabbing a stool by its leg and hurling it at Hua Xu, who dodged to one side and deflected the blow. My mother tried desperately to put herself between them. "I can't believe these outrageous things you've done!" my father cried.

Hua Xu was unabashed. "Revolution—that's what I've done."

At last my father managed to shove my mother aside. He charged, fists raised. Hua Xu turned tail and fled, but once he had reached a place of relative safety, he called back defiantly: "Revolution—that's what I've done!"

It made me hanker for revolution. Cultural Revolution or not, we primary school pupils were afraid of our teachers. If we talked or distracted others in class or if we got into a fight, they would often force us to write self-criticisms. I must have written more self-criticisms in primary school than I did compositions. And our teachers would then paste them up on the classroom walls, making us lose a lot of face. The exploits of Hua Xu and the other older boys gave us a sense that we wouldn't have to write any more self-criticisms once we got into middle school, for there it was not the pupils who were afraid of the teachers but the other way around. Once we got into middle school, we thought, misbehavior had a chance of gaining legitimacy as revolutionary action.

So it was that in the early summer of 1972 we crossed the new concrete bridge and entered the grounds of Haiyan Secondary School. Some students were playing basketball, and others lay sprawled on the grass, chatting away. As we passed the classroom buildings, we saw students sitting on almost all the windowsills. One of them beckoned us— a boy from our alley who was a year older than us. "Just got out of class, did you?" we asked.

He shook his head. "No, we're in the middle of class." He leaned out, pulled each of us up through the window, and introduced us to his neighbors.

We'd never seen anything like this. The classroom was buzzing with noise, with some pupils sitting on desks, others walking back and forth, and a couple locked in a furious argument, seemingly about to come to blows. A teacher stood on the rostrum, writing some physics problems on the blackboard. As he wrote, he explained some point or other, but not one of his pupils seemed to be listening.

This scene left us dumbfounded. We had to be missing something. We pointed at the teacher. "Who's he talking to?" we asked our friend.

"He's talking to himself."

We snickered. "You're not afraid of him?"

"Afraid of him?" He chuckled. "This is middle school, you know—it's not your primary school."

As he spoke, he rummaged around in the desk until he found a piece of chalk. He raised his arm and let fly. The teacher saw it coming and ducked out of the way, then carried on explaining the laws of physics, as though it was perfectly normal for pupils to target him for missile practice.

What is revolution? Now at last we knew.

差距
disparity

It's only a short step from cowardice to bravery—that's something I learned from a teenager many years ago. This was back in the mid-1970s, when amid many dreary strictures we reached the final stages of the Cultural Revolution. He was one of my high school classmates, and today he still lives in the town where we grew up; unable to hold down a job, he depends on his father's meager pension to make ends meet. The boy I remember had fine, delicate features marred by protruding teeth; with his puny, underfed frame, he would tag along in the rearguard as our gang roamed the streets.

We were eager for any kind of trouble in those days, picking fights with others our age, sometimes even plucking up courage to take on boys a good few inches taller than we were. When the action was at its thickest, this classmate would make sure he kept out of harm's way, looking on from a safe distance—not running away but not taking part in hostilities either. But one day he was transformed into a fearless hero, and thereafter he was always the first to throw himself into a fight and the last to beat a retreat.

Our gang had been bested that day by a pack of older youths, and we ended up fleeing from them in terror, clutching our heads. He raced home but soon came running back, kitchen cleaver in hand. On the way he paused for a moment and slashed his cheek with the blade. As blood poured from the wound, he daubed it freely over his face like warpaint and then, screaming at the top of his lungs, charged toward our adversaries.

They who had been chasing us so gleefully now found themselves confronted by a daredevil brandishing a kitchen cleaver, with blood streaming down his face. "The weak fear the strong," the Chinese saying goes, "the strong fear the violent, and the violent fear the reckless." Our vanquishers turned tail and fled, with the boy hot in pursuit, shouting, "I'll teach you who's boss now!"

The rest of us, who had been scurrying away in panic minutes earlier, took courage from his truculent display. We regrouped and charged after him, shouting, "We'll teach you who's boss now!" As we raced through the streets, in no time at all we were dripping with sweat, and in order to maintain speed and avoid getting winded, we soon abbreviated our battle cry to the snappier "Who's boss?"

That afternoon news of our exploit swept through the whole town, earning us celebrity as the Who's Boss Gang. After that, other young hooligans would greet us with obsequious smiles and the older boys would give us a wide berth. My classmate, having won our heartfelt respect, no longer tagged along behind us—overnight he had become the leader of the pack.

Why the sudden transformation? The reason was simple, so simple that today it hardly seems credible. One day his parents had gotten into an argument with the neighbors over some trivial matter, suspecting them of pinching their coal briquettes or something of the kind. The argument escalated into a full-blown fight, in which the boy too became involved. He chose to strike out at the weakest possible adversary he could find, the neighbors' pretty daughter, landing a punch right on her plump little breasts. That was all it took to make him a new man. Later he waved the palm of his hand before our envious eyes and recounted how his four happy fingers had—separated only by her blouse—established firm contact with her shapely bosom. His thumb, he said, had missed out on the treat, but his fingers had felt a heart-stopping softness.

That momentary feeling of ecstasy convinced my class-mate that he had already lived as long as he needed to. "I've had a feel of a girl's tits! I can die now," we often heard him say, a blissful smile on his face.

It was the conviction that he could now die without regrets that inspired this timid creature to feats of extraordinary daring. That's what our adolescence was like: momentary contact with a girl's breasts was a life-changing catalyst. Growing up in an era of extremes, we might be afraid of nothing when we were in the middle of a street fight, but we would tremble at the thought of a female body.

A second high school classmate—whose identity remains a mystery to this day—once scrawled on the blackboard the words "In love," an expression we understood intuitively, although we had never once used it. As the news spread, students in the other three first-year classes rushed over to view the inflammatory graffiti, although they were careful to wear sternly censorious expressions and shout "Let's catch the hooligan!" as they approached the classroom. Once in front of the blackboard, they gawked in awestruck silence, unable to tear themselves away. I myself had never seen these two words together, for the phrase had long disap-peared from popular usage, and to be suddenly confronted by it made the blood flow hot in my veins.

The two crudely written characters were allowed to remain on the blackboard for a good ten days, as incrimi-nating evidence, because the school's Revolutionary Com-mittee needed to track down the hooligan who had written them. First they had all the boys in our grade hand in their composition books so they could compare the handwriting. When this failed to produce a suspect, they scrutinized the composition books of all the girls, with an equal lack of success. The scope of the search was then extended to the second-years, again to no avail. In the end nothing came of it, and the Revolutionary Committee chairman had personally to purge the crime scene of the offensive language. For me this came as a big blow, since I had got into the habit of stopping to admire "In love" every time I went past, thereby slaking my thirst for romance. With its disappearance, even this vicarious satisfaction was impossible.

The anonymous classmate who wrote these words on the blackboard must surely have known that he was committing hooliganism, and so, we concluded, he must deliberately have written the characters in such a sloppy hand so that he could escape detection and get away scot-free. A popular film at the time had a line that went, "No matter how sly the fox, he's no match for the wily old hunter." After the "In love" episode, a new version of this line began to circulate among us: "No matter how wily the hunter, he's no match for the sly little fox."

My son has told me that in his middle school biology class the teacher directed the girls to sit on the boys' laps and then began to explain the physical differences between the sexes and the principles of sexual intercourse, pregnancy, and so on. After he had finished, one of the students raised his hand and asked, "Sir, is there a lab class, too?"

Thirty years ago, however, boys and girls in high school did not talk to one another. They would have loved to, of course, but did not dare. Even if they had a crush on a member of the opposite sex, the most they could do would be to cast furtive glances at them. The boldest boys might quietly slip notes to girls, but they wouldn't dare use words that clearly expressed love and instead employed elaborate circumlocutions, saying they wanted to give them an eraser or a pencil. The recipient would understand at once what game they were playing and react with unease, even fear. If the note was ever exposed to public view, the girl would feel deeply ashamed, as though she had done something improper.

Today high school students have no inhibitions about relationships, and the issue of teenage romance is discussed openly in society at large. In one video clip I have seen posted on the Internet, a boy sits on a school desk during recess and leans over to hug a girl sitting in the chair next to him. While classmates walk back and forth and talk about this and that, the couple kiss and cuddle as though they have the whole room to themselves. In a second clip, a boy falls to his knees in a school corridor and offers a bouquet of flowers to a girl. She brushes him aside and nips into the girls' bathroom. The boy hesitates for a second, then follows her into the bathroom, flowers in hand. These days pregnancies among high school girls have become so common they are no longer controversial, but it is still startling to find that some teenage girls actually show up for abortions in their school uniforms. I read that in one case the girl was escorted to the hospital by no fewer than four schoolboys. When the doctor said she needed a relative's signature, all four rushed forward.

What has made us move from one extreme to the other? Countless answers could probably be offered, but I doubt that such a cascade of responses will really provide a clear explanation. One point, however, is clear: when society undergoes a drastic shift, an extremely repressed era soon becomes a very lax one. It's like being on a swing: the higher you soar on one side, the higher you rise on the other.

China's high-speed economic growth seems to have changed everything in the blink of an eye, rather like a long jump that let us leap from an era of material shortages into an era of extravagance and waste, from an era when instincts are repressed into an era of impulsive self-indulgence. A quick jump seems to be all it took to cross a span of thirty years.

Just look at China today: the urban high-rises shooting up like forests under a gray and murky sky; the thick mesh of expressways, far outnumbering our rivers; the dazzling array of merchandise in shopping centers and supermarkets; the endless lines of traffic and pedestrians in the streets; the constant glitter of advertisements and neon signs; the nightclubs and massage parlors, beauty salons and foot-washing joints, lining every block; not to mention the luxury restaurants three or four floors high, each floor the size of an auditorium, rimmed on all sides by sumptuous private rooms, two or three thousand people all wining and dining, shiny-faced with satisfaction.

But just thirty years ago, before we took that leap, we saw no high-rises, apart from one or two in big cities like Beijing and Shanghai; we had no concept of expressways or advertisements; we had very few stores, and very little to buy in the stores we did have. We seemed to have nothing then, though we did have a blue sky.

Those were the days of the rationing system, when men were restricted to coupons for just twenty-seven pounds of grain per month and women to twenty-five, along with coupons for half a pound of meat and two ounces of oil per person. When you bought grain, you needed to hand over grain coupons along with your cash, just as when you bought pork and vegetable oil, you needed to pay in cash, meat coupons, and oil coupons. On top of that there were cotton coupons, which we combined with cash to buy cotton in the fabric shop, then went to the tailor's to get measured and fitted for a jacket or pants—although most people would try to save money by making their own clothes. There were no clothing factories then, and stores didn't sell ready-made clothes. If you had a sewing machine in your house, you would be the undying envy of all your neighbors.

In managing the household budget, we had to run the tightest of ships, restricting ourselves to nine ounces of rice a day, a few slices of pork a week, and ten drops of oil with each stir-fry, for only in that way could we avoid overspending our monthly allotment. In the world in which my generation grew up, we neither had enough to eat nor so little to eat that we would die of hunger. When we think back to what was best about our childhoods, we tend to reminisce about remarkably similar things, all involving the eating of some kind of treat; apart from that, we have very few memories to cherish.

We townsfolk seldom had anything left over, even if we reduced consumption to a minimum. For men it was practically impossible to fully satisfy one's appetite on twenty-seven pounds of grain a month; but women could typically manage with a little less than their ration, so they would use their leftover coupons to supplement the diets of their husbands or brothers. Oil coupons and meat coupons likewise failed to meet one's needs, so people would often buy coupons on the side to help maintain life and limb.

Peasants in my home district tended to have extra oil coupons in hand, for when they harvested rapeseed and delivered it to state-owned oil-pressing plants, the coupons would be their compensation. For them it was an important source of supplementary income. If they needed money to pay for medical treatment or a wedding, cash-strapped peasants would come into town and quietly sell their surplus coupons. In that era of public ownership, this was considered speculation and profiteering.

Inspired with a crusading zeal, some high school classmates and I formed a team of vigilantes to crack down on such activities. Today, I suppose, we would be described as volunteers, but volunteers at least can expect some free meals, and the only meal we got was if we opened our mouths wide and took a gulp of the raw winter wind. We would rouse ourselves at four in the morning to lie in ambush near the marketplace, hiding at street corners or behind utility poles, like hunting dogs poised for action. If we found someone selling oil coupons on the sly, we would leap out at him, confiscate his coupons, and march him off in triumph to the anti-speculation office.

We got a kick out of bullying those weaker than ourselves, believing too that we were performing a public service. Although we certainly had victories to our credit, our detainees tended to be peasants well past their prime, and the oil coupons we seized from them seldom amounted to very much. What's more, the peasants never dared resist, for they themselves were convinced they were doing something wrong, and so their only reaction was to weep helplessly as we snatched away their coupons.

We did, however, fight one epic battle against a strongly built young peasant. He was a good head taller than any of us, and his chest was as broad as two of us put together. When we threw ourselves on him, he fought back stubbornly. He clenched his right hand tightly into a fist but dared not actually punch us, for he knew that would simply aggravate his offense; all he did was shove us aside with his left hand and make a run for it. This was the fiercest resistance we had ever encountered, and he might have gotten away had we not had numbers on our side, to hem him in from all directions. It helped too that some classmates were armed with bricks, with which they banged him over the head, and soon we had him pinned down on the ground. Even so, he still had his right hand curled in a fist and still tried with his left hand to push us away. We knew he had to have coupons in his right hand, but we could not pry his fingers apart, no matter how hard we tried. Two boys pinned his arm tightly to the ground while another pounded his

fist with a brick until it was bathed in blood. Finally he
unclenched his hand, revealing a bunch of blood-soaked oil
coupons; counting them, we found a pound's worth altogether. After we had marched him to the anti-speculation
office, a thorough search revealed that he had an additional
eleven pounds of coupons hidden away in his clothes.

A full twelve pounds of oil coupons—this was our biggest bust ever. Under questioning, as he mopped his blood-
stained face, the young man confessed to speculation. In
order to pay for his wedding, he had borrowed nine pounds'
worth of coupons from friends and relatives, and the other
three pounds were the result of his family's scrimping and
saving: his parents and brothers and sisters had gone for half
a year without eating a drop of oil, making do with vegetables boiled in salted water.

That morning thirty-odd years ago retains a grim, appall-
ing clarity in my memory today. While we celebrated our
triumph with laughter all around, our victim recounted his
simple story with a grimace. Since he was a first offender, his
punishment took the form of confiscating his twelve pounds'
worth of coupons and making him write a pledge that he
would never again engage in such nefarious activity. As he
wrote the pledge, his injured right hand trembled—whether
from pain or from grief, I do not know. His fingers dripped
crimson, and the pledge of good behavior became a letter
written in blood.

So he was released, but we were not ready to let him off
so easily. We dogged and harangued him as he went on his
way, eager to show off in front of curious onlookers. To them
we would tirelessly relate the details of our twelve-pound
coupon haul, eliciting gratifying whistles of surprise. He
walked on amid our jeers, weeping openly without any trace
of embarrassment; sometimes he raised his right hand to
wipe away his tears, wincing with pain as he did so. We
didn't stop until we had walked right to the edge of town;

there we directed some last words of abuse at him and watched as he gradually disappeared in the distance along a country path. Clutching his injured hand to his chest, with a dazed and hopeless look on his face, he set out on the long road home that morning long ago.

It is with a heavy heart and a feeling of shame that I recall this episode now. I have no idea whether this decent young man went on to marry as he had planned, or how he managed to pay back those nine pounds' worth of coupons he had borrowed. What I remember most vividly is how, when we were beating him on the head, he controlled his rage and never fought back, just pushed us away with the palm of his hand.

Now, after all the dramatic changes in Chinese society, yesterday's profiteers have become today's small tradesmen. Urban unemployed and landless peasants, for their own survival, set out stalls in the city or ply their wares along the street. In Beijing alone, such people number in the tens of thousands. Unlicensed, they are highly mobile, and the local government is unable to levy revenue from them. At the same time, in the eyes of municipal officials, the appearance everywhere of these hawkers damages the city's image and detracts from "harmonious society." In response there has been created a Bureau of City Administration and Law Enforcement, whose intimidating officers fan out in all directions. If you walk along a street or cross a pedestrian bridge in Beijing, you will often find it lined with vendors squatting on the ground, hawking their cheap wares, and as soon as someone yells, "Here come the Admin!" you will see them hastily sweep up their merchandise and scuttle away.

Today's City Administration officials show little signs of progress in their ways of dealing with petty tradesmen, confiscating property as freely as we vigilantes did in the 1970s. Their spoils, of course, include items we could never have imagined back then. A few years ago, when I lived in an apartment near a Beijing subway station, I would often see unlicensed pedicab drivers picking people up or letting them off outside the station—and City Administration trucks loaded with confiscated pedicabs as well. I saw crushed looks on the faces of the dispossessed drivers, who had used all their savings and borrowed right and left to buy a pedicab, then pedaled the streets day and night, dripping with sweat in summer and winter alike, to support their families and pay for their children's schooling. When the pedicabs they depended on for their livelihood were confiscated, their futures were confiscated, too.

In recent years, as pedicabs, flatbed carts, and merchandise are regularly hauled away, relations between hawkers and city officials have become more and more hostile, sometimes leading to violent conflict. This never attracted much attention from society until a vendor named Cui Yingjie stabbed and killed a City Administration enforcer. With all the media coverage of the case, people began to realize that the crude confiscation of carts and merchandise is in effect a denial of the hawkers' right to a livelihood. As Cui Yingjie himself put it at his trial, after expressing remorse for what had happened, "All I wanted to do was to set up my own stall and try to change my life for the better."

After the stabbing, protective equipment became more sophisticated: City Administration officers were fitted out with smartphones, knife-proof vests, helmets, slash-resistant gloves, high-intensity flashlights, and so forth. Military police have been hired as instructors, to train the City Administration enforcers in practical techniques: how to seize a knife, how to extricate oneself when grabbed by the collar or the hair, how to dislodge a hand clamped around one's throat or waist.

Why did yesterday's profiteers and today's hawkers react so differently when their possessions were taken away from them? As times change and social mechanisms evolve, it seems to me, different survival instincts come into play. In social terms the Cultural Revolution was a simple era, whereas today's society is complex and chaotic. One of Mao Zedong's remarks sums up a basic characteristic of the Cultural Revolution. "We should support whatever the enemy opposes," he said, "and oppose whatever the enemy supports." The Cultural Revolution was an era when everything was painted in black and white, when the enemy was always wrong and we were always right; nobody had the courage to suggest that the enemy might sometimes be right and we might sometimes be wrong. Deng Xiaoping, in turn, said something that captures the zeitgeist of our current age: "A cat that catches the mouse is a good cat, no matter whether it's black or white." In so saying, he overturned Mao's system of values and pointed out a fact long evident in Chinese society: right and wrong often coexist in a single phenomenon and interact in a dynamic of mutual displacement. At the same time, his comment put an end to the argument about where socialism and capitalism belong in China's economic development.

So China moved from Mao Zedong's monochrome era of politics-in-command to Deng Xiaoping's polychrome era of economics above all. "Better a socialist weed than a capitalist seedling," we used to say in the Cultural Revolution. Today we can't tell the difference between what is capitalist and what is socialist—weeds and seedlings come from one and the same plant.

Sometimes a word's meaning moves from simple to complex and in so doing reveals a social change. "Disparity"* is just such a word.

In the 1970s, as far as city and town dwellers went, there were no obvious social disparities in China, but that didn't

*chaju

stop us from talking about disparity every day, denouncing hollow disparities in empty rituals. Everyone scrutinized his own thinking for inequalities, for gaps between himself and progressive individuals like the exemplary soldier Lei Feng.* "Study advanced models, note disparities"—such was the catchphrase of the day. Like novice monks reciting sutras, we would talk mechanically every day about "disparity," spinning our wheels in endless, hackneyed verbiage. In our compositions from elementary school through high school we would write over and over again how, under the guidance of the Lei Feng spirit, we were reducing ideological disparities, helping the old lady next door by bringing her water from the well. By my second year of high school our teacher of Chinese had taken as much as he could take. "You've all been fetching water for the old lady next door for ten years already," he said, rapping on the pile of essays stacked on his desk. "Why don't you change your example once in a while? How about fetching a sack of rice for the old man next door?"

Decades later we still talk endlessly about disparities, but no longer are they vacuous ideological disparities. Today they are real, down-to-earth social disparities; gaps between rich and poor, city and village; differences between regions; inequalities in development, income level, and allocation; and so on. Huge social disparities are bound to trigger mass protests and individual acts of resistance. When we beat that young peasant with bricks, he never once struck back with his fist; now when an official—without using any violence, just doing his job, enforcing regulations—simply confiscates a bicycle cart and the things on it, he is stabbed to death by the hawker. Why is this? I think it is because when "disparity" moves from narrow to broad, from empty

---

*Lei Feng, killed in a freak accident in 1962, aged twenty-one, was post-humously lionized as a devoted servant of Chinese socialism.

to real, it demonstrates how widespread are China's problems, how intense its contradictions.

During the socialist advances of the Mao era, although development was slow and economic returns were meager, social inequalities did genuinely contract. What Mao was never able to resolve was the gap between city and country. After thirty years of Deng Xiaoping's open-door policy, economic output has rapidly expanded: GNP has grown from 364.5 billion yuan in 1978 to more than 33 trillion yuan in 2009—almost a hundredfold increase. But the gap between city and country has not diminished; on the contrary, it has increased. According to official figures, the disparity between urban and rural residents' income has grown to a ratio of 3.33:1 or, in absolute numbers, by 9,646 yuan, the largest such gap since economic reforms began. The figures for 2009 have yet to be released, and official sources issue only vague acknowledgments that the gap is continuing to widen.

In May 2006, my friend Cui Yongyuan, an anchorman on China Central Television, began to retrace the route of the Red Army's Long March,* along with his film crew and twenty-six other people from different walks of life. It took them 250 days to travel the 3,800 miles, battling the elements through all four seasons, across snow-clad mountains and through endless grasslands, until their triumphant return to Beijing in January 2007. Cui Yongyuan came home with many tales, both happy and sad, and one day when we were together, he shared some with me. This is one of them:

By the summer of that year, just when the soccer World Cup finals were taking place in Germany, Cui's miniature

*The Long March is the name given to the arduous trek by Communist forces during the mid-1930s, when they escaped from encirclement by Nationalist troops in central China to a safe haven in the northwest.

Long March expedition arrived at an impoverished area in China's southwest, and there he had a sudden inspiration: to organize a soccer match for the local primary school children. Even if it was a far cry from the passions in Berlin, he thought, at least it would create a little ripple of World Cup excitement in this backward hinterland county.

He immediately encountered two problems. The first was that no soccer ball could be found in the stores of the county town, so he had to send two fellow Long Marchers off in a car to a bigger city to buy one. The second was that the local primary school children not only had never seen a soccer match; they had never even heard that such a game existed.

Cui Yongyuan located a large field—fields were one thing they did have there—and had a designer in his film crew put up a goalpost. A thousand children sat on the grass and watched attentively as Cui launched his crash course in elementary soccer. He began the lesson by demonstrating the penalty kick, placing the brand-new soccer ball on the penalty spot and proudly introducing his cameraman, the crew member with the most soccer experience.

The cameraman was used to playing without a referee and without an audience, so with the eyes of so many spectators upon him he naturally tensed up. Although he managed to strike a dashing enough figure in his run-up, he betrayed his amateur status in the delivery. The ball ballooned over the bar like a shell fired from a howitzer, painted a rainbow-like arc in the air, then hit the ground with a resounding thump and rolled into the middle of a cow pie.

Bowing his head in chagrin, the cameraman trotted over and retrieved the ball from the sticky pile of dung, carried it over to a pond nearby, gave it a good wash, then returned it to its place on the penalty spot. Cui Yongyuan now had the schoolchildren line up to practice taking penalties. An unforgettable scene ensued as each child kicked the ball, ran after it, waited till it stopped moving, picked it up, scampered over to the pond to give it a cleaning, then put it back on the penalty spot. Washing the soccer ball, they understood, was one of the basic rules of the game.

This—a true story—took place in the summer of 2006, when more than a hundred million Chinese watched the World Cup on television. World Cup matches were first broadcast in China back in 1978, the year when our soccer league was officially inaugurated. In the 2002 World Cup tournament, hosted jointly by Japan and Korea, the group match between China and Brazil was seen by 200 million Chinese. So in many parts of China today children have long been familiar with such brands as Nike and Adidas. Wearing school uniforms as they do, today's youngsters have little scope for making fashion statements, so—a Beijing schoolteacher informs me—they compete in showing off their footwear instead. If they are all wearing Nike basketball shoes, say, then it will come down to who is wearing which generation of Jordans or Kobes. Meanwhile, in southwest China, there are children who have never even heard of soccer.

During the 2008 Beijing Olympics many low-income Chinese longed to visit the "Bird's Nest" National Stadium and the "Water Cube" National Aquatics Center, symbols of the new China. They spent long days and nights journeying by train and long-haul bus, arriving in Beijing travel-worn but tingling with anticipation. Asking directions all the way from the station to Olympic Park, they longed to go in and explore, but entrance tickets to the park alone were in very short supply, and the tickets resold by scalpers were outrageously expensive. For security reasons, perhaps, people without tickets were banned from entering Olympic Park, so they had no choice but to stand a long way off and take a photo of themselves with the Bird's Nest and Water Cube in the distant background. Even so, their faces were wreathed in smiles.

At the same time there was no shortage of empty seats inside the stadiums—seats with excellent views of the events as well. High officials and big shots, being accustomed to an extravagant lifestyle, set no great store by the plum seats they had been given, never bothering to reflect that the tickets going to waste in their pockets would have been treasured by other Chinese. Nor did they give a second thought to the fact that such a multitude of ordinary people would travel so frugally to Beijing and then be unable to get their hands on even a basic sightseeing ticket for Olympic Park.

China today is a land of huge disparities. It's like walking down a street where on this side are gaudy pleasure palaces and on that side desolate ruins, or like sitting in a strange theater where a comedy is being performed on one side of the stage and a tragedy on the other.

When Louis Vuitton, Gucci, and other such luxury brands build huge outlets in the most glamorous streets of Chinese cities; when exhibitions of luxury goods are greeted with open arms in places like Shanghai, Guangzhou, and Shenzhen (where sales exceeded 200 million yuan in just a few days); then people suddenly realize that China has changed overnight from a luxury-goods processing site to a luxury-goods consumption center. The financial crisis may have caused sales of these goods to undergo a steep decline in the traditional European and American markets, but they remain hugely popular in China.

Since June 2008 luxury goods have been the weakest segment of retail sales in the United States. But in China, according to a recent report, sales of these goods grew by about 20 percent in 2008. By 2015, when sales are expected to maintain 10 percent annual growth, they may well surpass $115 million; this would make China the world's top consumer of luxury goods, with 29 percent of the world's total consumption. A study by China's Brand Strategy Association reported a development even more startling: Chinese consumers who can afford international name brands already number 250 million.

At the same time, poverty and hunger are still endemic in many parts of China, and there is no end to heartrending stories. Here is one that I heard: A long-unemployed husband and wife, out walking with their young son, pass a fruit stall. The boy sees that bananas are cheap and asks his parents to buy him one. But what little change they have in their pockets is not enough to buy a banana, so they hurry him on. The boy bursts out crying: it's been so long since he had a banana. He cries all the way home and keeps crying once he's home. His father, exasperated, hits him. His mother runs over, pushes the father away; they start to quarrel. The harsh words and the boy's unending cries suddenly overwhelm his father with despair. He hates himself, his uselessness, his joblessness, his empty pockets. He goes out on the balcony and throws himself off without even a backward glance. His wife screams, dashes out the door, down ten flights of stairs, kneels on the ground, cradles her husband's head, sobs, calls his name, feels his life leaving him. Minutes pass, she pulls herself together, sets the broken body down, presses the elevator button. Back in the apartment, her son still crying, she rummages around for a piece of cord, puts a stool in the middle of the room, ties the cord to a ceiling hook. Her son sits there watching, bewildered, so she jumps off the stool, turns his chair to face another way, climbs back on the stool, fastens the noose, and kicks away the stool.

Here's a second story: Another jobless couple, the daughter in primary school. She comes down with a fever; forehead scalding hot, she asks them to take her to the doctor.

They have no money, they tell her; they have to go out and look for work; they don't have time. She understands, she says just borrow a little money from a neighbor, she'll go see the doctor herself. Her father tells her mother to borrow the money, and she tells him the same; they start to argue. They've cadged so many loans and never been able to pay them back, they can't face the prospect of having to ask for more. Never mind, the girl says, she doesn't have to see a doctor. But she feels faint, she's not up to going to school; she'll have a nap in her room instead. Her father sets off on his job hunt; her mother stays to clean the kitchen. As she leaves, she checks to see if her daughter is asleep. When she pushes the door open, she finds the girl hanging by her red scarf, the one she patted flat before folding every night, that she tied carefully around her neck every morning, her favorite accessory.

There are many other such stories I could tell. It's not that I so relish stories of misfortune; rather, that Chinese realities are telling us these stories every day. Our realities, of course, tell us other kinds of stories, too. For example, there are already hundreds of thousands of Chinese whose disposable assets exceed 10 million yuan—825,000 of them, according to the latest *Hurun Report*. This figure includes 51,000 individuals with more than 100 million yuan, whose annual expenditure is said to average 2 million yuan.

Consider, in contrast, the following figures: if you define the poverty line in China as a 2006 income of 600 yuan or less, then there are 30 million Chinese living in poverty; if you raise the threshold to 800 yuan, there are a full 100 million. When I pointed this out at a talk in Vancouver in 2009, a Chinese student rose to his feet. "Money is not the sole criterion for judging happiness," he objected. This remark made me shudder, for it is not just a single student's view; a substantial number of people in China today would take a similar line. Surrounded by images of China's growing prosperity, they have not the slightest inclination to concern themselves with the hundred million who still struggle in almost unimaginable poverty. That is the real tragedy: poverty and hunger are not as shocking as willful indifference to them. As I told the Chinese student, the issue is not how we judge happiness but how we address a widespread social problem. "If you are someone with an annual income of only 800 yuan, you will earn a lot of respect for saying what you did," I replied. "But you're not."

In the past thirty years, China has developed at a remarkable pace, maintaining an average annual growth rate of 9 percent and in 2009 becoming the second-largest economy in the world. In 2010 China's revenues are set to hit 8 trillion yuan, and we are told proudly that we are on the verge of becoming the second-richest country in the world, trailing only the United States. But behind these dazzling statistics is another, unsettling one: in terms of per capita income China is still languishing at a low rank, one hundredth in the world. These two economic indicators, which should be similar or in balance, are miles apart in China today, showing that we live in a society that has lost its equilibrium or, as the popular saying has it, in a society where the state is rich but the people are poor.

Unequal lives give rise to unequal dreams. About ten years ago China Central Television interviewed Chinese youngsters on Children's Day, asking them what gift they would most like to receive. A boy in Beijing wanted a Boeing jet of his own, while a girl in the northwest said bashfully, "I want a pair of sneakers." Though much the same age, these two children were worlds apart in their dreams, and the girl is probably no more likely to get a pair of sneakers than the boy is to get his own plane. Such is China today: we live amid huge disparities between recent history and contemporary reality, and from one dream to the next. The comment from the student in Vancouver makes me feel these are disparities that Chinese society is perfectly prepared to accept.

I will tell one more true story to end this chapter, an episode set in one of China's southern cities. There, amid the myriad clusters of high-rise buildings and the packed shopping malls, a sixth-grader was kidnapped. The two kidnappers embarked on this crime in desperation, having hardly a penny to their names and no experience whatsoever in kidnapping. After getting nowhere in their search for employment, they decided to take matters into their own hands. Without planning or preparation, they seized a pupil on his way home from primary school one day, clapped their hands over his mouth, and dragged him, struggling, into an unused factory workshop. Then they asked the boy for his mother's mobile number, went to a callbox nearby, and delivered instructions about the ransom. They didn't realize they needed to call from some other place completely, and the authorities, tracing the call, quickly sealed off the area. Before long they were in police custody.

While waiting for the ransom to be delivered, the kidnappers ran out of money, so one of them went out and borrowed just enough to buy two box lunches, gave one to the boy, and shared the other with his accomplice. On his rescue, the boy told the police, "They're so poor! Just let them go, won't you?"

草根

grassroots

Five or six years ago a ritzy development began to go up in a bustling downtown area of one of China's main cities. When completed, it rose more than forty stories; its accommodations included six luxury apartments, each more than twenty thousand square feet in size and lavishly equipped with top-of-the-line kitchen and bathroom fixtures from well-known international brands. These hundred-million-yuan apartments were all snapped up as soon as they came on the market, and the first person to purchase one was not a celebrated real estate agent, financial investor, or information-technology baron but an inconspicuous actor on China's economic stage: an impresario of blood sales or, in common parlance, a blood chief. This wealthy blood chief was such a free spender he purchased the apartment outright with a single payment. It is a good place to begin my story of the grassroots.*

In my novel *Chronicle of a Blood Merchant*, published in 1995, I drew on childhood memories to create a character named Blood Chief Li. At that time "grass roots" in Chinese simply meant "roots of grass," but within a few years we imported from English a new meaning, and in China

*caogen

163

"grassroots" has come to be used in a broad sense to denote disadvantaged classes that operate at some remove from the mainstream and the orthodox.

I remember as a child seeing a man pay peasants for giving blood at the hospital. He dressed in a white coat just like a doctor, but it was always grubby, with dirty gray stains on its elbows and seat; a cigarette invariably dangled from the corner of his mouth. Among prospective blood vendors he was known simply as Blood Chief, and he exercised unquestioned authority over his empire of blood. Although his status in the hospital was lower than that of the most ordinary nurse, he had a profound grasp of the benefits that accrue from steady, daily accumulation, and over the passage of years he quietly confirmed his standing as a king of the grassroots. In the eyes of the peasants who, from poverty or from some yet more dire cause, had come forward to sell blood, he was sometimes even seen as a savior.

Hospitals in those days had well-stocked blood banks. From the start he made the most of that circumstance, planting seeds of uncertainty in the minds of the blood vendors as they journeyed from afar, sparking anxiety as to whether they would be able to find a buyer for the blood flowing in their veins. And he effortlessly cultivated their respect so that it came straight from their hearts, and on that basis he imparted to these simple country folk an understanding of the importance of gifts. Although most of them were illiterate, they knew that interaction is essential to one's relationships with others. Through him they came to realize that gifts not only are the most vital prerequisite for interaction but actually constitute an alternative language, one predicated on a certain degree of personal loss but also able to communicate such sentiments as favor, homage, and esteem. Thus he made them understand that, before leaving home, they should make a point of picking up a couple of heads of cabbage, or a few tomatoes and a handful of eggs. When they presented to him their cabbages, tomatoes, or eggs, they would be paying him a compliment and addressing him with deference, whereas if they arrived empty-handed, this would be to forfeit language and lose the power of speech.

For decades he managed his kingdom with unstinting devotion. Then times changed: hospital blood banks began to encounter shortages, blood purchasers had to fawn on blood vendors, and the authority of hospital blood chiefs was undermined. But this did not worry him in the least. He was now retired and took advantage of the opportunity to become a real blood chief, no longer affiliated with a hospital in the traditional manner.

This blood chief passed away some ten years ago, but before he died, he pulled off an amazing feat. In late 1995 my father, who had just finished reading *Chronicle of a Blood Merchant,* told me over the phone that the blood chief had found a way to greatly boost his retirement income. As China's market economy began to thrive, the chief discovered that blood prices differed from one region to another, and in short order he organized close to a thousand blood vendors to travel some three hundred miles, through a dozen different counties, all the way from Zhejiang to the county in Jiangsu where he knew blood commanded the highest price. His followers thereby increased their earnings, and his own wallet bulged like a ball that's just been pumped up.

What an epic journey that must have been! I have no idea how he managed to induce this band of misfits, all strangers to one another, to form such a motley grassroots crew. He surely must have established some code of discipline, emulating a military chain of command and conferring limited powers on a dozen or so members of this untidy rabble, authorizing them to give free rein to their respective talents, whether threats or cajolery, flattery or curses. His officers kept those thousand foot soldiers in line, while he simply needed to oversee his dozen officers.

Their collective enterprise bears some resemblance to the operations of a mobile infantry unit during wartime, or perhaps a religious pilgrimage in full swing, as this dense mass of humanity clogged up long sections of highway. Men argued and women gossiped, clandestine affairs were conducted, and the unlucky were laid low by sudden illness. No doubt there were touching cases too of mutual support, or true love coming to fruition. You would be hard put to find anywhere a throng of people as colorful and diverse as this ragtag army of grassroots blood vendors.

If my childhood blood chief had not died so early, he would surely have accumulated enough wealth to move into a luxury apartment too, although he was not, of course, in the same league as the blood chief in the big city, who exercised even greater authority and is said to have commanded the loyalty of a hundred thousand blood vendors. Such is Chinese reality today: although blood vendors must hand over a percentage of their earnings to their boss, they still make more money than if they were to sell blood independently.

This big blood chief enjoys an opulent lifestyle under an assumed name, and nobody knows just how big a fortune he has. Whenever blood bank reserves run low, all the big hospitals eagerly seek his services, and sometimes he is so heavily booked that it can be impossible to set up a dinner date. To him business is business, and he will make sure that the blood he controls flows in the direction of whichever hospital offers the best price for his product.

Blood selling, which seems such a humble and demeaning profession, turns out to be just the kind of story on which *Forbes* magazine would love to do a feature: a quintessential rags-to-riches story. Another such tale concerns a trash recycler sometimes known as the Beggar Chief but more often dubbed the Garbage King. Although he is Garbage

King in only one district of one municipality, he has managed to amass a fortune in the many millions. In Chinese cities every residential neighborhood has people who specialize in recycling trash; they buy cheaply items that the residents plan to throw away and, after sorting, sell them at a slightly higher price to bigger recyclers—like the Garbage King. After jacking up the prices, he resells the waste to manufacturers, enabling them to save on raw materials. When this millionaire Garbage King was interviewed, he struck a modest, unassuming pose. How had he discovered this business opportunity? the reporter wondered. "I just did the things nobody else was willing to do," he replied.

This straightforward answer reveals a secret about China's economic miracle. Chinese people today, inspired by a fearless grassroots spirit, have propelled the economy forward by seizing every possible opportunity. So it is that our economic life is full of kings: the Paper Napkin King, the Socks King, the Cigarette Lighter King, and so on. In Zhejiang there is a Button King who oversees a button range so extensive it boggles the mind. The profit on a single button may be minuscule, but so long as people go on wearing clothes, there'll be a demand for his buttons everywhere in the world. The same goes for paper napkins, socks, and cigarette lighters: however humble such products may be, the minute they claim a significant market share, they are perfectly capable of becoming an empire of wealth.

A man I know runs a BMW dealership in the city of Yiwu. One day he was visited by an old man from the countryside, with a dozen or more children and grandchildren clustered around him. They all tumbled out of a van and bustled their way into the dealership, and the younger members of the family began to select a car for the well-heeled patriarch. A BMW 760Li with a sticker price of more than 2 million yuan caught his eye. "Why is this car so expensive?" he asked. But when the dealer listed all its advanced features and technological refinements, the old man just shook his head and said he couldn't understand a word. Finally the dealer pointed at the driver's seat. "It took two cows to make this," he said. "The leather is cut only from the finest part of the hide."

The old peasant, who as a boy had tended cattle long before he struck it rich, was won over right away. "If two cowhides were used just for one seat, this has to be a top-of-the-line vehicle!" he marveled. He bought the 760Li for himself and assigned cars in the BMW 5 series to his sons and daughters-in-law and cars in the 3 series to the youngest generation. When it came time to pay for their purchases, his family toted in several large cardboard boxes from the van, each filled to the brim with cash. The paterfamilias had no confidence in checks and credit cards; for him only currency notes counted as proper money.

On the basis of his life experience and simple, down-to-earth way of thinking, the old man immediately understood why the BMW 760Li was so expensive. Some Chinese grassroots may get involved in business without any knowledge of economics or any management experience, but they are perfectly capable of getting rich quick, thanks to their distinctive personal outlook on things. Just as the old man had his way of appreciating the 760Li, the grassroots way of thinking—even if it seems a lot like that of a country bumpkin—can enable one to get to the heart of the matter in no time at all.

With all the changes since 1978, there's no end to such stories. China's economic miracle of the past thirty years, it's fair to say, is an agglomeration of countless individual miracles created at the grassroots level. China's grassroots dare to think and dare to act; in the tide of economic development they will adopt any method that suits their purposes, and they are bold enough to try things that are illegal or even criminal. At the same time China's legal system has developed only slowly, leaving plenty of loopholes for the grassroots to exploit and putting all kinds of profits within their reach. Add to that their dauntless courage, which comes from their having nothing to lose, since they began with nothing at all. "The barefoot do not fear the shod," the Chinese say, or as Marx put it, "The proletarians have nothing to lose but their chains, and they have a world to win."

If you look at the names that appear on the recent wealth rankings in China, almost all of these multimillionaires have come up from the grass roots. These honor rolls tell stories of sudden upswings—of empty-handed paupers transformed overnight into multimillionaires, of the glory and wealth that partner fame and fortune. At the same time they recount tales of sudden ruin, showing how disgrace follows glory and how wealth can vanish in the blink of an eye. Judging by the *Hurun* Rich List, during the past ten years there have been no fewer than forty-nine grassroots tycoons who either have been arrested or have fled to avoid arrest. Their crimes come in all shapes and sizes: misappropriation of funds, conspiracy to rob, conspiracy to swindle, corporate bribery, fabrication of financial bonds, illegal diversion of public funds, irregular seizure of agricultural land, contract fraud, credit certificate fraud, and so on. No wonder the Rich List is popularly known as the Pigs-for-Slaughter List. In China there's a saying, "People fear getting famous just as pigs fear getting fat," reflecting the observation that fame invites a fall just as a fattened pig invites the butcher. On the other hand, as Rupert Hoogewerf (aka Hu Run), the creator of the Rich List, has noted, "Pigs that deserve to die will die, whether or not they make it onto the rich list."

In November 2008 Huang Guangyu, who rose from humble beginnings in a small Guangdong village to become known as the wealthiest man in China, was arrested by Public Security on a charge of gross financial misconduct. After the launch of Guomei Electronics in 1987, within ten years he had developed it into the country's largest household appliance retailer. In 2008 he was listed as the richest man in China for the third time, with personal wealth of 43 billion yuan. In May 2010 a court found him guilty of "illegal operations," insider trading, and bribery and sentenced him to a fourteen-year prison term. Several years ago, when Huang Guangyu topped the Rich List for the first time, he was asked by a journalist, "This Richest Man title of yours—did you have to pay for it?"

"Hu Run pisses me off," Huang replied. "Why would I give him money? That list of his is like an arrest warrant—whoever's on it ends up in big trouble!"

The Rich List—or the Pigs-for-Slaughter List, if you prefer—is just the tip of the iceberg in China today. Off the list, in the ubiquitous battle for economic advantage, many more grassroots are performing their own dramatic rises and staggering falls. Or, as Chinese bloggers like to say, most pigs get slaughtered even before they're fattened up. And on today's stage, which lurches so unpredictably from comedy to tragedy, none of us has any idea when our end will come.

When we look back at the Cultural Revolution and all the political infighting it involved, there's no end to the stories of those who rose swiftly from the grassroots, only to drop like a stone afterward.

In August 1973 something unexpected happened at the Tenth Congress of the Chinese Communist Party. It was no surprise that Mao Zedong sat in the central chair on the presiding bench or that Premier Zhou Enlai sat on his right, but everyone was amazed to see a mere thirty-eight-year-old sitting on Mao's left. After Mao announced the opening of the congress and Zhou read the political report, this newcomer calmly began to read the "Report on the Revision of the Party Constitution."

His name was Wang Hongwen, and at the start of the Cultural Revolution he had been simply a security guard at a Shanghai textile mill. In November 1966 he and a few other workers set up what soon became a famous militant organization, Shanghai Workers' Revolutionary Rebel Headquarters. After that he enjoyed a meteoric rise, and in less than seven years he was elevated from a night watchman to a vice premier in the Politburo, No. 3 in the hierarchy after Mao and Zhou.

But good times don't last long, and just three years later—after Mao died and as the Cultural Revolution ended—he became a prisoner along with the other members of the so-called Gang of Four: Jiang Qing, Zhang Chunqiao, and Yao Wenyuan. In their show trial in December 1980 this celebrated revolutionary rebel was sentenced to life imprisonment for crimes that included "organizing and leading a counterrevolutionary clique."

In China's overheated political campaigns, revolution was just a short step away from counterrevolution. In popular idiom it was a matter of "flipping pancakes": everyone was just a pancake sizzling on the griddle, flipped from side to side by the hand of fate. Yesterday's revolutionary became today's counterrevolutionary, just as today's counterrevolutionary would become tomorrow's revolutionary.

After that Wang Hongwen was gradually forgotten. Left to stew alone in his prison cell, he could only sigh and moan at the thought of his fleeting days of glory. Wracked by liver cancer, he came to a desolate end; when he died, in August 1992 at the age of fifty-seven, only his wife and brother attended his cremation.

How many stories of rebels' topsy-turvy careers did the Cultural Revolution tell? Too many to count, and way too many to mention. If all these stories were laid out one after another, they would stretch as endlessly as a highway and be as hard to tally as the trees in a forest.

This makes one think of Liu Shaoqi, who died wretch-
edly in the early Cultural Revolution. After many months of
humiliation and abuse at the hands of militants, this former
head of state died in November 1969, at the age of seventy-
one. So much time had passed since his last haircut that his
white locks dangled down to his shoulders, and his naked
corpse was covered only with a single sheet. In the ledger
recording the storage of his ashes his occupation was given
as "Unemployed."

During the Cultural Revolution, as I moved from childhood to adolescence, the grim reaper twice made special
visits to our town. The first was right at the beginning,
when Communist Party officials, once so awesome, were
denounced as capitalist-roaders and some chose death
rather than subject themselves to further mistreatment. The
second was when the Cultural Revolution ended: the rebels who had ruled the roost for ten years suddenly became
followers of the Gang of Four, and it was their turn to be
purged. Some felt the end of the world was nigh and, like
the capitalist-roaders ten years earlier, took their own lives
by this means or that.

One of the leading militants in our county during the
Cultural Revolution, having risen precipitously from the
grassroots, threw his weight around every chance he could.
When I was young, I would often see him at struggle sessions; and when his voice blasted from the loudspeakers,
it sounded like two or three voices overlaid on top of each
other. As he read out his denunciations, he would keep an
eagle eye on the row of capitalist-roaders, with their heads
bowed, and if one of them made the slightest movement,
he would break off his tirade and kick the unlucky victim
fiercely in the back of the legs to bring him to his knees.
When Mao Zedong set up "three-in-one" revolutionary
committees with a mix of veteran cadres, military men, and
Red Guard militants, this activist secured a place on the

county revolutionary committee and was soon promoted to the rank of deputy chief, confirming his legitimacy in the new order. When he walked the streets of our town, everyone vied to claim acquaintance with him and hailed him with a warm, respectful greeting; but he would respond simply with a perfunctory nod, a reserved expression on his face. If we children hailed him with a cheery "Chief," however, he would wave to us in a friendly way.

After the Cultural Revolution he was placed in solitary confinement during the campaign to purge followers of the Gang of Four. My classmates and I had just graduated from high school then; feeling at loose ends, our curiosity piqued, a few of us went to observe his interrogation. We knew he had been shut up in a little room behind the department store warehouse, so we clambered up on top of the wall just outside and sat there with our legs dangling. Through an open window we could see him sitting on a stool, facing two questioners on the other side of a table. They banged the table and harangued him just as mercilessly as the rebels had interrogated capitalist-roaders. This militant, once so intimidating, was now a broken man, abjectly confessing all the crimes he had committed as a lackey of the Gang of Four. He started crying at one point, breaking off from the recitation of his misdeeds to mention that his mother had died just a few days earlier. It upset him terribly that he could not attend the wake, and suddenly he wailed as loudly as a child, "My mom was spitting blood! She filled up a whole washbasin with it!"

This simply provoked his interrogator further. "Don't talk nonsense!" he barked, rapping the table. "How could your mom have so much blood?"

One morning when the guard was in the toilet, the man made good his escape, fleeing along the seawall for a good five miles before he finally came to a stop. There he stood, gazing blankly at the boundless sea, oblivious to the waves crashing on the shore. Head bowed, he walked over to a corner shop, stood at the counter for a minute, and emptied all the cash out of his pockets. He bought two packs of cigarettes and a box of matches, then returned to the seawall.

Peasants who were working in the fields nearby noticed how he lingered there, chain-smoking steadily. When he had finished both packs, he watched in a daze as they went about their jobs, then turned, scrambled down the embankment, and threw himself into the seething waves. By the time his captors closed in on his location, there was no sign of him, just a heap of cigarette stubs on the seawall. It wasn't until several days later that his body washed up on a beach farther along the coast. His corpse was so swollen, I heard, that it was hardly recognizable. He was still wearing shirt and trousers, but shoes and socks had been scoured away.

The Cultural Revolution induced grassroots from society's underbelly to throw caution to the winds, and in a revolution where "to rebel was justified" they gained opportunities to soar. Completely ordinary people enjoyed such rapid vertical elevation that they were said to have "taken off in a helicopter." With the end of the Cultural Revolution these people slipped from their lofty perches and found themselves in free fall, plunging through the grassroots layer to the level below, where only jailbirds roosted. "What goes up comes down even quicker" was the new line used to mock these rebels on the slide.

Of course there were even more people whose rises and falls followed a less dramatic trajectory. In the town where I lived there were a number of such cases, and I will now introduce one of them.

After the January Revolution of 1967 swept across China and government seals everywhere exchanged hands, rebels and Red Guard organizations that had failed to snatch control of official seals were not reduced to total despair, for it occurred to them that they could simply carve their own. Thus self-appointed grassroots power structures popped up everywhere in dazzling array, like the Tang poet's evocation of the scene after a snowstorm: "Spring seems to stretch as far as the eye can see/Pear blossoms bloom white on tree after tree."

It was against this backdrop that our hero rose to prominence, establishing an Invincible Mao Zedong Thought Publicity Team, with himself as its self-proclaimed leader. He must have been about forty years old then. In the past he had been a timorous creature and a man of few words. He was not the sort who swaggered along in the middle of the street; rather, he kept his eyes cast down as he walked and tended to hug the wall. Even children could push him around.

At first it was the older boys in the alley who would give him a hard time, just to show off. As he walked past, a boy would veer into his path and deliver a stinging body check. His reaction was simply to stand still, scowl at the boy who knocked into him, and then walk off without a word. I admired those older boys for being so bold as to bully a grown-up, and later on we preschoolers worked up the courage to harass him too, tossing pieces of gravel at him as he passed. He would turn and throw us a dirty look, then walk on without saying a word. This made us feel on top of the world, and we reveled in our newfound power.

When the roiling tide of revolution swept our way, people were quick to attach themselves to one rebel organization or another. This meek, self-effacing individual found the temptation impossible to resist and eagerly offered his services to the cause. Perhaps because he seemed so unprepossessing, the rebel organizations wrote him off as lacking revolutionary fiber and rejected his application for admission. Helpless and desperate, he resorted to establishing his own one-man rebel organization. He had an Invincible Mao Zedong Thought Publicity Team seal carved and hung it impressively from his waistband.

Thus began his days of excitement and distinction. I remember that every time he appeared on the streets of our town, his jacket was always stuffed inside his trousers—the only person in the whole town to wear his clothes that way—for this rendered his seal all the more conspicuous. A whistle hung from a string around his neck, and in his hand he clutched a copy of *Quotations from Chairman Mao* as he strutted back and forth, head held high and chest thrown out, his eyes scanning the people in the street. Often without warning he would give a blast on his whistle, and when the passersby stopped to look at him, he would clasp his Little Red Book in both hands. "Everyone turn to page twenty-three. We will now read a passage by Chairman Mao," he'd loudly instruct.

In those days most people carried a Little Red Book with them at all times; as soon as they heard his summons they pulled their books out of their pockets and, at his prompting, earnestly began to read aloud quotations of Chairman Mao. After finishing page twenty-three, they would find he had other pages earmarked for them to read—pages forty-eight, fifty-six, seventy-nine, and more—until he judged it time to bring their pious study session to a close. "That's all for today," he would solemnly declare, closing his copy of the Little Red Book. "I trust you'll all continue your reading when you get home."

"Yes, we will," the passersby would answer, relieved to have recovered their freedom.

Some people were deeply embarrassed that their failure to carry the Little Red Book had been exposed to the world, but he did not take them to task for being so remiss. "Just don't forget the Little Red Book tomorrow," he said amiably.

With this ideological policeman on the loose, everybody

made sure to take the Little Red Book with them when they went out. As soon as his whistle blew, the resounding peals of Mao Zedong's quotations would echo along the street.

We children no longer took liberties with him, assuming mistakenly that only the biggest rebel leader around would be able to bring so many militants and ordinary towns-people to heel with a single blast of his whistle. We didn't realize he was basking in borrowed glory, for in those days everyone was easily cowed by the Little Red Book.

We became his admirers. Other rebels didn't give us a second glance, but he was very willing to establish cordial ties with us. We would swarm around as soon as he appeared and tag along behind as he walked down the street. We also followed his sartorial lead and tucked our jackets inside our pants, although—much to our disappointment—we had no seals to hang from our waistbands. He was generous enough, however, to allow us a feel of his Invincible Mao Zedong Thought Publicity Team seal and would stand in the street with a patient smile on his face no matter how long we spent fingering it. But when we pushed things a bit too far and asked whether we could hang this wonderful seal from our waistbands for a moment, he would sternly refuse. "That would amount to a power seizure," he warned.

This rebel without a clique enjoyed good relations with the townsfolk. Schools no longer offered classes and facto-ries no longer operated shifts—everyone was too busy mak-ing revolution to go to work—so some thought they might as well take the opportunity to travel and visit family and friends in other parts of the country. As long as they had a letter of introduction from a revolutionary rebel organiza-tion, they did not need to pay for their ticket or hotel room, so they would turn to the one-man propaganda team for help. He greeted such suppliants warmly and never turned anybody down. To meet the growing demand, he kitted himself out with another revolutionary prop: a faded military satchel strung over his shoulders, stuffed with a thick sheaf of mimeographed letters of introduction.

At the top of the letter were printed the words "Supreme Directive" and underneath was a quotation of Mao Zedong's: "We hail from all corners of the country and have joined together for a common objective. . . . All people in the revolutionary ranks must care for each other, must love and help each other." A standard form letter followed.

He was thrilled every time someone asked him for a letter of introduction. He would plop himself down on the ground, take a blank sheet out of his satchel, and rest it on his thigh. "Where is it you want to go?" he would ask, then conscientiously jot the answer down. Each time he would issue two letters, one authorizing free transportation, the other authorizing free lodging. Then he would produce from his pocket a tin of red ink paste, untie his belt, and detach his Invincible Mao Zedong Thought Publicity Team seal, dip it in the ink paste, and carefully impress it on the paper.

Later, owing to an unfortunate mishap, his life in the fast lane screamed to a halt. One day he must have been in a rush when going to the bathroom, and when he pulled down his pants a little too vigorously, his Invincible Mao Zedong Thought Publicity Team seal slipped off his waistband and tumbled into the cesspit below. As luck would have it, a Red Guard was using the bathroom too, and trouble followed. The seal was famous throughout our town, and everyone knew that the characters for "Mao Zedong Thought" were carved on it. "What, you dropped 'Mao Zedong Thought' in the cesspit?" the Red Guard cried, scandalized.

In a second, life's high tide suddenly began to recede. After delivering his scolding, the Red Guard never brought the matter up again. But the guilt-stricken publicist subjected himself to endless self-reproach. His jacket was no longer tucked inside his trousers, and the satchel over his shoulders was no more to be seen. The whistle still hung

from his neck, but when he gave it a halfhearted blow and
passersby respectfully brought our their Little Red Books,
expecting to read Mao's quotations aloud under his supervi-
sion, he would simply burst into tears and slap himself
in the face, denouncing himself as a counterrevolutionary.
"I deserve to die a thousand deaths!" he cried in distress. "I
dropped 'Mao Zedong Thought' down the toilet."

The passersby with their outstretched Little Red Books
were stunned, and it took a few moments for them to understand what had happened. Naturally they felt it incumbent
on them to sternly criticize his faux pas; the fashion of the
day, after all, was to advertise one's revolutionary standpoint
at the earliest opportunity, whatever the circumstances. But
nobody seriously considered him a counterrevolutionary,
and since everyone knew him to be a decent fellow, he was
never subjected to a struggle session.

But he continued to blow his whistle and heap abuse on
himself in public, to the point where passersby got quite
annoyed. One day somebody reached his limit. "A counterrevolutionary like you," he cursed. "What makes you think
you've got the right to blow that damn whistle at us all the
time?"

The whistle-blower turned pale as a sheet. "I'm so sorry,"
he said, bowing his head penitently. "This won't happen
again."

When he next appeared, a whistle no longer hung from
his neck. He had changed his outfit and now was wearing a
papier-mâché dunce cap on his head and clutching a broom
in his hand. He would spend the whole day sweeping the
streets of our little town, fearing that some awful retribution might descend on his head at any moment.

As time passed and the Cultural Revolution ended, the
man reverted to his original self, passing his days in quiet
obscurity, and nobody paid the slightest attention to him if
they passed him in the street. With that he was completely

forgotten by our little town. When I went back home a few years ago and mentioned this man to some of my childhood companions, not one of them could remember him, and when I recounted these stories that left such an impression on me, they looked so surprised it was as though this was the first time they had ever heard them. I tried to jog their memories, stressing how he would blow his whistle and orchestrate readings of Mao's quotations. Finally it rang a bell with one of them, and he promised to make some inquiries. A couple of days later he came by to report that the man had died ten years earlier. "He's blowing his whistle in the underworld now," he chuckled, "leading the lost souls in a recital of Mao Zedong's selected sayings."

I looked baffled. "He kept his whistle lovingly all those years," my friend explained, "and his dying wish was to have it deposited with his ashes." In keeping with age-old conceptions of death as an extension of life, he had asked for his most cherished possession to accompany him into the next world, for use whenever needed.

For him, I realized, the whistle signified the most vital symbol of his existence. Without the Cultural Revolution, there would have been no whistle, and no ups and downs. Although his rise and fall can hardly be compared to Wang Hongwen's, he did in his own way scale a peak, only to tumble off the other side. If on his deathbed he thought back to those glorious days when he could blow his whistle and lead everyone in a reading of Mao's quotations, he would have felt, I'm sure, some satisfaction at a job well done.

As I look back over China's sixty years under communism, I sense that Mao's Cultural Revolution and Deng's open-door reforms have given China's grassroots two huge opportunities: the first to press for a redistribution of political power and the second to press for a redistribution of economic power.

山寨

copycat

The story of contemporary China can be told from many different angles, but here I want to tell it in terms of the copycat, a national myth playing itself out on a popular level.

The word here rendered as "copycat"* originally denoted a mountain hamlet protected by a stockade or other fortifications; later it acquired an extended meaning as a hinterland area, home to the poor. It was also a name once given to the lairs of outlaws and bandits, and the word has continued to have connotations of freedom from official control.

In the past few years, with the increasing popularity of copycat cell phones that offer multiple functions at a low price, the word "copycat" has given the word "imitation" a new meaning, and at the same time the limits to the original sense of "imitation" have been eroded, allowing room for it to acquire additional shades of meaning: counterfeiting, infringement, deviations from the standard, mischief, and caricature. With visas such as these one can gain entry to the Land of Imitation and take up residence in Mountain Hamlet. It would not be going too far to say that "copycat"

*shanzhai

181

has more of an anarchist spirit than any other word in the contemporary Chinese language.

Copycat cell phones began by imitating the functions and designs of such brands as Nokia, Samsung, and Sony Ericsson; to muddy the waters further, they gave themselves names like Nokir, Samsing, and Suny Ericcsun. By plagiarizing existing brands and thereby skimping on research and development costs, they sold for a fraction of the price of established products; given their technical capabilities and trendy appearance, they soon cornered the low end of the consumer market.

With the rapid growth of the copycat industry there is now a dizzying variety of knockoff phone brands. One has recently appeared in the stores under the mantle of Harvard University. Claiming to be manufactured by "Harvard Communications," the brand presents President Obama as its spokesman and sports a beaming Obama on its advertisements. His smile, seen everywhere these days, has to count as the most famous—and the most powerful—smile in the world, but now it's been hijacked and made to appear in promotions for Chinese copycat cell phones. "This is my Blackberry," Obama tells us with a grin, "the Blockberry Whirlwind 9500!"

Obama is today's symbol of that long-running American dream, but I am pretty sure he could never have imagined such an outlandish misuse of his image, and Americans at large would no doubt be flabbergasted to see their president serving as brand ambassador for a Chinese knockoff. We Chinese take it all in our stride, for we don't see anything wrong with copycatting Obama. After all, in China today, with the exception of the party in power and our current government leaders—plus retired but still living party and state leaders—everybody else can be copycatted and ridiculed, imitated and spoofed, at will.

Thirty-three years after his death, Mao Zedong—our

erstwhile Great Leader, Great Teacher, Great Commander, and Great Helmsman—like Obama came to play the starring role in a Chinese copycat advertisement. On October 1, 2009, the sixtieth anniversary of the founding of the contemporary Chinese state, a karaoke parlor in Zhejiang posted two huge red banners on either side of its door. On them Mao Zedong appeared in military uniform and cap, with microphone in hand, belting out a song; he looked nothing like the charismatic leader of the revolutionary era and much more like the kind of petty bureaucrat who haunts nightclubs at all hours of the night. In the bottom right corner were listed such patriotic anthems as "China, Today Is Your Birthday," "My Motherland," "China, I Love You," and "O People of China." "We put the poster up on October 1," one of the staff proudly explained. "It's our way of marking this great national celebration."

In 2008 Mao's home province of Hunan embarked on a campaign to select Mao look-alikes from all over the country. Lured by such tempting bait, surely plenty of tourist fish would throw themselves on the hook; visitors would flock to Hunan and line its coffers with a more ample store of legal tender. "This is an innovation in our cultural system reform," a local official explained. "It will effectively promote the development of our cultural tourism industry."

One hundred and thirty Mao Zedong look-alikes traveled from all corners of the country, braving every hardship to arrive at their destination. After several elimination rounds thirteen finalists entered the last stage of the competition. At the news conference they sat in a row on the stage, each with a fake mole stuck on his chin. Some struck the classic pose of the historical Mao Zedong, a cigarette between their curled fingers and an ankle resting on their knee. The real Mao Zedong spoke with a genuine Xiangtan accent; copycat Xiangtan accents spilled from the mouths of the copycat Maos. Most were dressed in Mao jackets of gray or green; one wore a replica of the octagonal cap in which Mao was photographed during the Long March; the others had their hair styled in the backward sweep that Mao favored. All at different stages in life, they declared that they represented Mao Zedong at varying stages in his career: the Jinggang Mountains version, the Long March version, the 1949 founding ceremony version. . . . One was so confident in his appearance that he refused to put on makeup; another put on makeup but claimed to be "the most physically unaltered." A third mock Mao, facing the packed audience below, improvised as giddily as a pop singer. "I'm a hundred and fifteen this year," he declared, clutching the microphone tightly, "but it gives me such a lift to be here, I feel just as young as you see me!"

Yet another Mao Zedong look-alike imitated Mao's speech at the founding ceremony: "Greetings, comrades!" His phony Xiangtan accent enlivened the atmosphere, and the audience cried happily in return, "Greetings, Chairman Mao!"

"Long live the people!" he continued.

"Long live Chairman Mao!" the crowd roared.

These past few years Mao Zedong has been copycatted constantly. In the most bizarre instance, a female Mao impersonator appeared in southwest China, making such an immediate impact that she was hailed by the Chinese media as "sweeping aloft in majesty," a literary expression over which Mao once claimed exclusive rights. When this fifty-one-year-old woman made herself up as Mao Zedong and walked along the street, waving to the crowds that gathered, she looked uncannily like the Mao who waved to the parading masses from Tiananmen, and the crowds pressed toward her, rushing to be the first to shake her hand. In a moment the street was a dense throng of humanity, and it took her more than half an hour to walk just a few hundred yards.

Everybody felt that this female copycat was even more

like Mao than the male impersonators they had seen. Of course, the cost to her personally and financially was far higher, for she had to invest enormous effort to master Mao's accent and mannerisms to the point where she could resemble him so closely in every way. Each time she made herself up to look like Mao it took her four hours and cost her 2,000 yuan in cosmetic expenses. To conceal her deficiencies in the stature department, she wore the highest possible elevator shoes. The real Mao was six feet tall, and she was not quite five foot six. After careful viewing of newsreel footage and endless hours perfecting the simulation of Mao's accustomed gait, this female copycat Mao Zedong managed to walk with her thickened insoles in such a way that people who saw her thought she looked just like Mao strolling along in his flat cotton shoes.

Once copycat cell phones had taken China by storm, copycat digital cameras, copycat MP3 players, copycat game consoles, and other such pirated and knockoff products came pouring forth. Copycat brands have rapidly expanded to include instant noodles, sodas, milk, medications, laundry detergent, and sports shoes, and so the word "copycat" has penetrated deep into every aspect of Chinese people's lives. Copycat stars, TV programs, advertisements, pop songs, Spring Festival galas, Shenzhou 7 space capsules, and Bird's Nest national stadiums have all made a splash on the Internet, each revealing their own special flavor and gaining instant popularity.

Copycat stars appear in imitation shows, just like the ersatz Mao Zedongs. The difference is that sham Maos require a physical likeness, whereas the copycat stars aspire merely to a similarity in spirit. However different their looks, so long as they can capture a star's voice and expression, they can achieve their goal and create some buzz. As their reputation soars, some copycat stars chafe at their limited resemblance to their models and end up wanting to look like them, too; so they go to enormous expense and suffer the discomfort of surgery to have themselves cosmetically reshaped, looking forward to the day when they and the stars they are imitating will look like twins. Fired with feverish ambition, they long to elevate themselves from copycat status to genuine article and to downgrade the original to a wannabe.

Copycat pop songs and copycat TV programs are even more varied, combining imitation with parody. Lyrics are altered at will so that the solemn becomes comical and the refined becomes crude, and the songs are deliberately performed out of tune. Copycat TV programs, released as videos on the Internet, tend to be send-ups of official TV programs, and China Central Television's *Network News* at seven o'clock each evening, notorious for its rigidity and dogmatism, has become a perennial target of mockery. In one spoof, two completely unfamiliar anchors appeared on our monitors in a skit inspired by the 2008 milk-powder scare. In the ponderous tones of *Network News* they announced that the regular anchors had been poisoned by contaminated milk and rushed off to intensive care; they had been brought in at the last minute to deliver that evening's broadcast.

Some versions of *Copycat News* have been quite incisive in confronting sensitive social issues. When official media outlets hem and haw, *Copycat News* gets straight to the point, telling things as they are and adding liberal doses of derision and sarcasm. After the tainted-milk scandal was exposed, it became clear that it was not just the Sanlu Group in Shijiazhuang whose infant formulas had astronomical levels of melamine; many other producers' infant formula exceeded the limits to varying degrees. China's entire milk industry suffered a major blow. Nobody would buy domestically produced milk powder, and many people stopped drinking milk. *Copycat News* had plenty to say about this.

It poked fun at Sanlu and the other milk producers, who were said to register their dissatisfaction with Sanlu in the following terms: "We put melamine in our milk powder, but you guys put milk powder in your melamine. Damn it, you're even more shameless than we are!"

In August 2008, after the success of the opening ceremony at the Beijing Olympics, the official Chinese media sang its praises to the skies, proudly declaring that such a glorious opening ceremony had no parallel in the past and would never be matched in the future. *Copycat News* said the same thing, but cynically. Its commentary went like this: "Such a glorious opening ceremony has never happened before and will never happen again. Why so? Because other nations with so many people do not have so much money, and other nations with so much money do not have so many people, and other nations with so much money and so many people do not have so much power."

China Central Television's annual Spring Festival gala provides the best possible chance for budding entertainers to make their name overnight. A decent female singer normally earns only about a thousand yuan for a day's work; but after she makes an appearance at the Spring Festival gala, she can ask a much higher fee—ten or twenty thousand yuan for a single song. The result is that to get a place on the gala program becomes a life-or-death struggle for many performers. They pull out all the stops, begging businessmen to underwrite them, imploring leaders to intercede on their behalf; sex is traded for money, or power. The gala keeps growing and growing, giving the director endless headaches: space needs to be found for more and more items on the program; there are fewer solos and many more ensembles.

A few years ago the following joke made the rounds: One of the top brass at CCTV decides that it is high time the gala was pared down. In order to ensure its artistic quality, he thinks to himself, they are just going to have to step on a few toes. He pulls out the drawer in which he has been keeping all the instructions, requests, and pleas he has received, dumps them all on the top of his desk, and studies them carefully one by one, scanning the signatures of the various bigwigs who have thrown their weight behind one or another performer. No, this one he can't afford to offend, nor that one either. In the end he is left with just three messages he can get away with ignoring—for they are all notes he himself has written to the director. He removes these three pieces of paper from the pile but then has second thoughts. "Why give myself a hard time?" he asks, and tosses them right back in.

It is against this backdrop that copycat variety shows are broadcast on the last evening of the traditional Chinese year, the same time as the official CCTV gala. In 2009 more than a dozen such copycat events were broadcast on the Internet. As Spring Festival approached, their organizers unleashed a flood of copycat advertising, sending vehicles out into the streets to publicize their events, conducting news conferences in city squares, marching through downtown holding aloft wastepaper baskets emblazoned with promotional quips. Advertising slogans for the copycat galas took multiple forms; one, borrowing Mao Zedong's calligraphy, had the line: "The People's Gala—for the people and by the people." Viewers who are fed up with the CCTV gala—young people in particular—turn off their televisions on the last night of the year and flick on their computers. As they eat and drink, they can relish on the Internet the copycat galas produced by the grassroots.

From this we can see that the copycat phenomenon has a certain positive significance in China today. Seen in this way, it represents a challenge of the grassroots to the elite, of the popular to the official, of the weak to the strong.

More than twenty years have passed since the Tiananmen protests of 1989, and from today's perspective their greatest impact has been the lack of progress in reforming the political system. It's fair to say that political reform was taking place in the 1980s, even if its pace was slower than that of economic reform. After Tiananmen, however, political reform ground to a halt, while the economy began breakneck development. Because of this paradox we find ourselves in a reality full of contradictions: conservative here, radical there; the concentration of political power on this side, the unfettering of economic interests on that; dogmatism on the one hand, anarchism on the other; toeing the line here, tossing away the rule book there. Over the past twenty years our development has been uneven rather than comprehensive, and this lopsided development is compromising the health of our society.

It seems to me that the emergence—and the unstoppable momentum—of the copycat phenomenon is an inevitable consequence of this lopsided development. The ubiquity and sharpness of social contradictions have provoked a confusion in people's value systems and worldview, thus giving birth to the copycat effect, when all kinds of social emotions accumulate over time and find only limited channels of release, transmuted constantly into seemingly farcical acts of rebellion that have certain anti-authoritarian, anti-mainstream, and anti-monopoly elements. The force and scale of copycatting demonstrate that the whole nation has taken to it as a form of performance art.

When, on the eve of the Beijing Olympics, the Olympic torch arrived in Chinese territory, the cities among which it was relayed were dictated by official fiat, and every torch-bearer was chosen meticulously by government officials. The cost may have been exorbitant, but the cities selected felt honored, and every torchbearer chosen felt proud. A small mountain village in Henan's Hui County clearly did not qualify for such glory, but the locals went ahead and organized for themselves a homegrown version of the relay, passing from one person to the next a simple handmade torch. Every villager was qualified to participate; no government approval was required. They all looked pleased as punch, for their love of China was not in the least inferior to that of the official torchbearers', and when footage of their exploit began to circulate on the Internet, it got a rapturous reception.

Because the West often criticizes China for its degradation of the environment, the Chinese government made a point of declaring the Beijing Olympics a green Olympics. But the official torch relay in China did not give me any sense that the Olympics were green. Led by police cars, the torchbearers would trot slowly along a road lined with crowds, and after the event the city streets were piled with garbage. With the relay in Hui County, on the other hand, I did get a taste of a green Olympics: no car exhaust, no carbon dioxide emissions from overexcited crowds, just villagers with their handmade torches trotting over the spring hills as a mild breeze blew and the sun shone brightly.

Copycat phenomena are everywhere in China today, and even the political arena, so long untouchable, has suffered an invasion. When the National People's Congress and the National Political Consultative Conference were in session, a man from Yibin in Sichuan, who described himself as a "Copycat Delegate to the National People's Congress," introduced several motions on the Internet regarding such issues as insurance, old-age pensions for peasants, and personal income tax, hoping for a wide airing of his ideas. His election was laced with black humor, for he explained that he had been the unanimous choice at a family gathering—a sardonic commentary on the government's practice of carefully vetting potential candidates for election to the NPC and NPCC. Although his election was the outcome only of a family get-together, this copycat delegate actually reflected more of a democratic spirit than those official delegates, for he won votes from relatives sincere in their support, not votes rigged by the authorities.

There are even more brazen and outrageous cases of copycatting: some people have adopted copycat tactics to transfer features of China's humorless political system to its dissolute sex industry. Last year I read on the Internet a jaw-dropping feature about a highly successful sex business in one of China's southern cities. The young women employed there were distinguished for their good looks and provided unstinting service to their clients, who unanimously praised the establishment as "top in the nation, first-class in the world." Why so? It was all due to excellent managerial practices, apparently. The boss had introduced a system that forged a bond between sex and politics, borrowing from the Chinese Communist Party and Communist Youth League their system of branch organization, his theory being that progressive role models had an important role to play in the purveying of sexual services.

In China, if one wants to enter the Communist Party and the Communist Youth League, one must undergo careful inspection and rigorous procedures. This sex-industry entrepreneur, having no affiliation with either the party or the Youth League, set himself up as a copycat Party Committee secretary and established under his banner both a "party branch" (women well versed in sexual services) and a "youth-league branch" (unseasoned new recruits), with the understanding that once the youth-league members gained more experience and positive endorsements from their clients, they could be promoted to full-fledged party members. Applying the time-honored methods of Chinese political organizations, he was able to enhance his employees' work ethic and at the same time have them supervise one another's performance. At regular intervals he would hold "organizational life" retreats for both categories of staff, where they conducted criticism and self-criticism, studied "superior methods" and identified "areas for improvement," learned how to "maximize assets" and "address deficits," so that the quality of their services could scale even greater heights.

This real-life-sex-entrepreneur/copycat-party-secretary has also imported the Communist Party's "advanced worker" category into his management structure, electing every month an advanced worker who has distinguished herself in terms of the number of clients serviced and adding her photograph to the array of top earners listed in the honor roll. In conventional honor-roll photographs in China you always see standard poses and healthy, purposeful smiles. In this copycat honor roll, by contrast, the snapshots look much more like the glossy pictures of starlets you see in fashion magazines, every one of the copycat advanced workers vying to attract attention with a simpering smile or a smoldering glance.

The social fabric of China today is shaped by a bizarre mixture of elements, for the beautiful and the ugly, the progressive and the backward, the serious and the ridiculous, are constantly rubbing shoulders with each other. The copycat phenomenon is like this too, revealing society's progress but also its regression. When health is impaired, inflammation ensues, and the copycat trend is a sign of something awry in China's social tissue. Inflammation fights infection, but it may also lead to swelling, pustules, ulcers, and rot.

As a product of China's uneven development, the copycat phenomenon has as many negative implications as it has positive aspects. The moral bankruptcy and confusion of right and wrong in China today, for example, find vivid expression in copycatting. As the copycat concept has gained acceptance, plagiarism, piracy, burlesque, parody, slander, and other actions originally seen as vulgar or illegal have been given a reason to exist; and in social psychology and public opinion they have gradually acquired respectability. No wonder that "copycat" has become one of the words most commonly used in China today. All of this serves to demonstrate the truth of the old Chinese saying: "The soil decides the crop, and the vine shapes the gourd."

Four years ago I saw a pirated edition of *Brothers* for sale on the pedestrian bridge that crosses the street outside my apartment; it was lying there in a stack of other pirated books. When the vendor noticed me running my eyes over his stock, he handed me a copy of my novel, recommending it as a good read. A quick flip through and I could tell at once that it was pirated. "No, it's not a pirated edition," he corrected me earnestly. "It's a copycat."

That's not the only time something like this has happened. In China today, in some spheres there is still a lack of freedom, while in others there is so much freedom it's hard to believe. More than twenty years ago I could say whatever came into my head when I was interviewed by a journalist, but the interview would undergo strict review and be drastically edited before publication; ten years ago I began to be more circumspect in interviews, because I discovered that newspapers would report everything I said, even my swear words; and now I am often amazed to read interviews I have never given—remarks that the reporter has simply concocted, a gushing stream of drivel attributed to me. Once I ran into a reporter who had fabricated just such an interview and I told him firmly, "I have never been interviewed by you, ever."

He responded just as firmly: "That was a copycat interview."

I was speechless. But that is our reality today: you may have done something illegal or unconscionable, but as long as you justify yourself with some kind of copycat explanation, your action becomes legitimate and aboveboard in the courtroom of public opinion. There's nothing I can do about it, except pray that in the future, when people make up conversations with me, they don't make me talk too much nonsense. If somebody has me say something clever, I'm even prepared to say thank you.

Last October I went on a quick tour of several European countries, sleeping in a different bed practically every single night, and when I got back to Beijing at the end of the month, I felt completely drained. What with jetlag as well, I was in quite a wobbly state for a couple of days, often imagining I was still in Europe. At one point I turned on my computer and did a little surfing on the Internet; soon I came across a copycat news item, one that announced the pregnancy of Prof. C. N. Yang's wife.

Chen-Ning Yang, a Nobel laureate in physics, has been a staple of copycat news reports ever since 2004, when at the age of eighty-two he married Weng Fan, then twenty-eight. Now copycat correspondents had concocted this story of his wife being pregnant, a development allegedly revealed by Yang in an interview. Many of the remarks attributed to him were quite absurd—like his saying with a smile that the unborn child had already been proven to be his. That is exactly the kind of fanciful invention I know so well, because in copycat interviews I often say equally ridiculous things.

For me this spurious report served a useful purpose, for after two days in a trance I was suddenly clearheaded once more, in no doubt at all that I was back in China.

If we conceptualize the copycat phenomenon as a form of revolutionary action initiated by the weak against the strong, then this kind of revolution has happened before in China—in the Cultural Revolution forty-four years ago.

When in 1966 Mao Zedong proclaimed, "To rebel is justified," it triggered a release of revolutionary instincts among the weaker segments of society, and they rebelled with a passion. Everywhere they rose up against those in positions of authority. Traditional Communist Party committees and state organizations totally collapsed, and copycat leadership bodies sprouted up all over the place. All you needed to do was to get some people to back you, and overnight you could establish a rebel headquarters and proclaim yourself its commander-in-chief. Soon there were too many copycat organizations and too little power to go around, triggering violent struggles between the various rebel headquarters. In Shanghai the struggle involved guns and live ammunition; but the rebels there were outdone by the ones in Wuhan, who used artillery pieces to assail each other's positions. In efforts to expand their power bases, copycat leaders fought incessantly in conflicts that differed little from the tangled warfare between bandits that was once so common in China. Eventually the victors would incorporate the remnants of the vanquished and emerge with enhanced authority. Once the traditional bases of party and state control had been eliminated, revolutionary committees—representing the new power structure—were soon established, and those copycat commanders who had triumphed in the chaotic factional struggle all of a sudden transformed themselves into the revolutionary committees' official heads.

Why, when discussing China today, do I always return to the Cultural Revolution? That's because these two eras are so interrelated: even though the state of society now is very different from then, some psychological elements remain strikingly similar. After participating in one mass movement during the Cultural Revolution, for example, we are now engaged in another: economic development.

What I want to emphasize here is the parallel between the sudden appearance of myriad rebel headquarters at the beginning of the Cultural Revolution and the rapid emergence of the private economy: in the 1980s, Chinese people replaced their passion for revolution with a passion for making money, and all at once there was an abundance of private businesses. Just as the copycat challenges the standard, so too the private sector assailed the monopoly status of the state-owned economy. Innumerable businesses soon went belly-up, only for countless others to take their places, just like the constant setbacks and dynamic comebacks associated with revolution, or like Bai Juyi's lines about the grassland: "Though burned by wildfire, it's never destroyed/ When the spring winds blow it grows again." China's economic miracle was launched in just this way. Through its continual cycles of ruin and rebirth the private sector demonstrated its enormous capacity for survival, at the same time forcing ossified, conservative state enterprises to adapt to the cutthroat competition of the marketplace.

In their colorful history during these past thirty years, the grassroots have performed feats unimaginable to us in the past, doing things their own way, through different channels. In Western terms, "all roads lead to Rome," and in Chinese terms, "when the eight immortals cross the sea, each displays his special talent." Their roads to success were highly unconventional, and so too were their roads to failure; the social fabric they have created is equally peculiar. Just as the reveille wakens soldiers from sleep, so too, as "copycat" took on a rich new range of meanings, it has suddenly brought into view all manner of things that have been churning below the surface during these years of hectic development. The awesome spectacle that has ensued is rather akin to what would happen if, in a crowded square, someone yells "Copycat!" in an effort to catch a friend's attention and everybody in the square comes dashing over, because that is the name they have all adopted.

As miracles multiply, desire swells. Tiananmen Gate, the symbol of Chinese power, and the White House, the symbol of American power, have naturally become the structures most vigorously emulated by copycat architects all across China. There is a difference, however. Mock Tiananmens tend to be erected by local officials in the countryside: newly prosperous villages convert their local government offices to miniature Tiananmens so that when the lowest-level officials in the Chinese bureaucracy are ensconced inside, they can savor the beautiful illusion of being masters of the nation. Imitation White Houses, on the other hand, supply office space for the rich and also meet their living needs. By day a company executive sits at his desk in a copycat version of the Oval Office, directing the activities of his employees by telephone; by night he takes his pretty secretary by the hand and leads her into the copycat Lincoln Bedroom.

In the course of China's thirty-year economic miracle many poor people from the grassroots have acquired wealth and power and have begun to hanker after a Western-style aristocratic life; moving into spacious villas, traveling in luxury sedans, drinking expensive wines, wearing designer brands, and saying a few words of English in an atrocious accent. As copycat aristocrats proliferate, so too do the social institutions catering to their needs: aristocratic schools and aristocratic kindergartens, aristocratic stores and aristocratic restaurants, aristocratic apartments and aristocratic furniture, aristocratic entertainments and aristocratic magazines. . . . In China there is no end of things claiming an association with aristocracy.

Here's a true little anecdote about one such copycat aristocrat. He built himself a luxury villa complete with swimming pool even though he couldn't swim, his theory being that no rich man's villa would be complete without a pool. At the same time he wasn't happy seeing the pool going to waste, so he used it to raise fish, which—steamed, braised, or fried—could be served up on his dinner table each day. It then occurred to him that five-star hotels have a particular name for their most elegant and extravagantly appointed rooms. So soon a bronze plaque appeared on the door of the master bedroom, inscribed complacently with the words

"Presidential Suite." Such is the lifestyle of China's nouveau riche.

Finally I need to relate my own copycat story.

In China in the olden days, dentists were in much the same line of work as itinerant street performers and more or less on a par with barbers or cobblers. In some bustling neighborhood they would unfurl an oilskin umbrella and spread out on a table their forceps, mallets, and other tools of their trade, along with a row of teeth they had extracted, as a way of attracting customers. Dentists in those days operated as one-man bands and needed no helper. Like traveling cobblers, they would wander from place to place, shouldering their load on a carrying pole.

I, for a time, was their successor. Although I worked in a state-run clinic, my most senior colleagues had all simply switched from plying their trade under an umbrella to being employed in a two-story building; not one of them had attended medical school. The clinic staff numbered not much more than twenty, and tooth extractions were the main order of business. Our patients, mostly peasants from the surrounding countryside, did not think of our clinic as a health-care facility but simply called it the "tooth shop." This name was actually quite accurate, for our small-town clinic was very much like a shop. I entered as an apprentice, and for me extracting teeth, treating teeth, capping teeth, and fitting false teeth were simply a continuous series of learning tasks. The older dentists we all referred to as "gaffers," for there were no professors or unit heads such as you would find in a full-blown hospital. Compared with the career of a dental physician, now such a highly educated profession, my job in the "tooth shop" was that of a shop-worker, plain and simple.

My training was overseen by Gaffer Shen, a retired dentist from Shanghai who had come to our clinic to make a bit of extra money—or "bask in residual heat," as we used to say. Gaffer Shen was in his sixties, a short and rather portly man who wore gold-rimmed spectacles and kept his sparse hair neatly combed.

The first time I saw my mentor-to-be, he was extracting a patient's tooth; but because he was getting old and had to strain with all his might to tug on the forceps, he was grimacing so painfully you might have thought he was trying to pull his own tooth out. The clinic director introduced me as the new arrival. Gaffer Shen nodded guardedly, then told me to stand next to him and watch as he used a cotton swab to daub the next patient's jaw with iodine and injected a dose of Novocain. Then he plopped himself down in a chair and lit a cigarette. When he had smoked it down to the butt, he turned to the patient and asked offhandedly, "Is your tongue big yet?"

The patient mumbled something in the affirmative. Gaffer Shen rose slowly to his feet, picked a pair of forceps out of his tray, and set to work on the diseased tooth. He had me observe a couple of extractions. Then he sat down in his chair and showed no sign of planning to get up again. "I'll leave the next ones to you," he said.

I was a bundle of nerves, for I still had only a rudimentary understanding of how to extract a tooth, and here I was suddenly at center stage. But I remembered at least the first two steps with the iodine and the Novocain, so I awkwardly instructed the patient to open his mouth wide and managed clumsily to complete the procedure. The patient watched me with a look of complete terror, as though one-on-one with a crocodile, which made my hands shake all the more.

As I waited for the anesthetic to take effect, I didn't know quite what to do with myself. But Gaffer Shen handed me a cigarette and suddenly became quite genial, asking me what my parents did and how many siblings I had. All too soon my cigarette was finished and the conversation was over. Thank goodness I was able to recall the next line of the script, and in my best imitation of Gaffer Shen I turned to the patient and asked, "Is your tongue big yet?" When he said yes, I was struck with horror at the prospect of what now lay ahead, and a chill ran down my spine. There was no way to get out of extracting that unlucky tooth, and I also had to put on a show of knowing exactly what I was doing and avoid making the patient any more suspicious.

That first extraction is something I will never forget. I had the patient open his mouth wide and fixed my eyes on the tooth that had to be pulled. But when I glanced into the tray and saw a whole line of forceps, all of different sizes and shapes, I was struck dumb, clueless as to which one I should use. I hesitated, then slunk back to Gaffer Shen with my tail between my legs. "Which forceps?" I asked in a low voice.

He got up, shuffled forward a couple of steps, and peered inside the patient's gaping mouth. "Which tooth?" he asked. At that point I was still vague about the names for the various teeth, so I just pointed with my finger. Gaffer Shen took a squint, pointed at a pair of forceps, then plopped himself back down in his chair and picked up his newspaper.

At that moment I had an intense sensation of being locked in a lonely, daunting struggle, without allies or sympathizers. I didn't dare look into the patient's staring eyes, for I was even more petrified than he was. I picked up the forceps, inserted them into his mouth, maneuvered them into position, and took a firm hold of the tooth. By a stroke of good fortune, it was already quite loose; all I needed to do was grip the forceps tightly and rock the tooth back and forth a couple of times, and it came straight out.

The real difficulty came when I was working on the third patient, for part of a root broke off inside his jaw. Gaffer Shen had no choice but to remove his foot from his knee and let the newspaper slip from his hand, rise from his chair, and come personally to attend to it. To clean out a root is much

more trouble than a simple extraction, and Gaffer Shen was
dripping with sweat by the end of it all. It was only later,
when I knew how to deal with this kind of complication,
that he could begin to enjoy a true life of leisure.

Our office had two dental chairs. I would usually call in
two patients at once, have them sit down in the chairs, and
then, as though dispensing equal favors to two trust beneficiaries, smear some tincture of iodine in their mouths and
inject them both with a dose of anesthetic. In the dead time
that followed I would take a nicotine break, and when my
cigarette was finished, I would ask, "Is your tongue big yet?"

Often both patients would answer at the same time, "Yes,
it's big." As though enforcing further terms of the trust, I
would pull out their teeth one after another and then move
on to the next two cases.

In those days Gaffer Shen and I coordinated seamlessly.
I made myself responsible for calling in the patients and
attending to their diseased teeth, while my mentor stayed
put in his chair, making notations in their medical records
and writing out prescriptions; only if I ran into trouble
would he personally take to the field. As my skills in tooth
extraction grew more accomplished, Gaffer Shen was called
to the front line less and less often.

Many years later I became an author. Western journalists were always curious about my dentist past, astonished
that with only a high-school graduation certificate and having had no medical education whatsoever I had proceeded
directly to tooth extractions. I groped around for an explanation that would make some kind of sense. "I used to be a
barefoot doctor," I would tell them.

Barefoot doctors were an invention of the Mao era: peasants with a smattering of education were shown how to perform routine medical procedures and then sent back home
with a medical kit on their backs. Why were they called
barefoot doctors? Because for them practicing medicine

was just a sideline activity; their basic work remained going out to the fields and laboring in their bare feet. When peasants around them came down with some minor injury or illness, they would be in a position to provide basic treatment on the spot, or if the case was serious, they would see the patient off to the hospital.

I knew it wasn't really correct to say I'd been a "barefoot doctor," for though I couldn't claim to have received much more training than those peasant doctors, I had at least been engaged in dentistry full-time. The problem was that for many years I couldn't find the right word to describe my first job, and it's only with the emergence of new vocabulary in China today that I can finally give Western reporters a more accurate picture of my situation. "I used to be a copycat dentist," I tell them now.

忽悠

bamboozle

What is 忽悠?* Originally it meant "to sway unsteadily"—like fishing boats bobbing on the waves, for example, or leaves shaking in the wind. Later it developed a new life as an idiom particularly popular in northeast China, derived from another phrase that sounds almost the same: 胡诱—"to mislead." Just as variant strains of the flu virus keep constantly appearing, 忽悠 has in its lexical career diversified itself into a dazzling range of meanings. Hyping things up and laying it on thick—that's 忽悠. Playing a con trick and ripping somebody off—that's 忽悠, too. In the first sense, the word has connotations of bragging, as well as enticement and entrapment; in the second sense, it carries shades of dishonesty, misrepresentation, and fraud. "Bamboozle," perhaps, is the closest English equivalent.

In China today, "bamboozle" is a new star in the lexical firmament, fully the equal of "copycat" in its charlatan status. Both count as linguistic nouveau riche, but their rises to glory took somewhat different courses. The copycat phenomenon emerged in collectivist fashion, like bamboo shoots springing up after spring rain, whereas "bamboozle"

*huyou

had its source in an individual act of heroism—the hero in question being China's most influential comedian, a north-easterner named Zhao Benshan. In a legendary skit performed a few years ago, Zhao Benshan gave "bamboozling" its grand launch, announcing to the world:

> *I can bamboozle the tough into acting tame,*
> *Bamboozle the gent into dumping the dame,*
> *Bamboozle the innocent into taking the blame,*
> *Bamboozle the winner into conceding the game.*
> *I'm selling crutches today, so this is my aim:*
> *I'll bamboozle a man into thinking he's lame.*

In "Selling Crutches" he proceeds with infinite guile, trapping the fall guy in one psychological snare after another, exquisitely employing deception and hoax to lead him down the garden path until in the end a man whose legs are perfectly normal is convinced he's a cripple and purchases—at great expense—a shoddy pair of crutches.

When this very funny routine was performed in CCTV's Spring Festival gala—the most-watched television program in China—the word "bamboozle" immediately took the nation by storm. Like a rock stirring up a tidal wave it triggered a tsunami-style reaction as phenomena long existent in Chinese society—boasting and exaggerating, puffery and bluster, mendacity and casuistry, flippancy and mischief—acquired greater energy and rose to new heights in bamboozle's capacious ocean. At the same time a social propensity toward chicanery, pranks, and other shenanigans drew further inspiration from it. Once these words with negative connotations took shelter under bamboozlement's wing, they suddenly acquired a neutral status.

Zhao Benshan put "bamboozle" on the lips of people all over the country, male and female, young and old. The word slipped off their tongues as smoothly as saliva and shot from their mouths as freely as spittle. Politics, history, economics, society, culture, memory, emotion, and desire—all these and more find a spacious home in the land of bamboozle- ment. It has become a lexical master key: in the palace of words it opens all kinds of doors.

Bamboozlement, of course, does not always have nega- tive connotations. When one is in a nostalgic mood, "bam- boozle" can serve to purge the word "trick" of its pejorative meaning. My mother is a case in point.

In an effort to eradicate snail fever in the late 1950s, Mao Zedong organized doctors and nurses in cities and towns into medical teams known as epidemic prevention brigades. They were sent to impoverished areas that lacked health care, where they treated snail-fever patients for free. My father was then living in the beautiful city of Hangzhou, where he had a job in the provincial-level epidemic preven- tion station. In his whole life my father spent only six years in school, three under the instruction of a traditional private tutor and three at a university; he acquired the rest of his education when studying on his own as a medic in the Com- munist armed forces. He laid claim to a dictionary as a tro- phy of war, and as the army marched south, he memorized new vocabulary on the go. His unit fought its way down to the southeastern province of Fujian, and afterward he made his way back to Hangzhou, where he transferred to the local hospital. There he met a nurse—later my mother. She urged him to study mathematics, physics, and chemistry; through assiduous effort he gained admission into Zhejiang Medical School, where he completed his three years' formal train- ing. After graduation he had no desire to continue working at the epidemic prevention station, for his dream was to be a surgeon. But he had no authority to choose his own career, and when the leadership assigned him to the epidemic pre- vention station, he had no choice but to go.

It was in this context that my father joined the epidemic

prevention brigade, which he saw as his first step to becoming a surgeon. Fired by this burning ambition, he thought it a necessary sacrifice to pursue his career away from Hangzhou. Arriving as brigade leader in Jiaxing, fifty miles northeast of Hangzhou, he hoped to transfer to the local hospital, but the Jiaxing authorities proposed instead to make him dean of their nursing school. He refused and headed instead for a smaller town on the coast, Haiyan. There a county hospital had just been built, and it needed a surgeon. At last his dream could come true.

In Haiyan Hospital my father's talents were given free rein, and he was kept busy removing infected spleens from victims of snail fever. This was a major operation: in city hospitals it was always the job of abdominal surgery specialists, and the grueling procedure could take up to seven or eight hours. In Haiyan my father would remove four or five spleens a day, and as he became more adept, he could do the job in just three or four hours. Meanwhile my mother continued to live with me and my brother in Hangzhou. She worked in the refined environment of Zhejiang Hospital and had no wish to leave Hangzhou and its lovely West Lake.

Every day, once he'd got a few spleens out of the way, my father would sit down in the little office adjoining the surgery and write to my mother on prescription stationery, extolling the beauties of Haiyan as though it were heaven itself. I never had the chance to read this correspondence, but after I made my home in Beijing and began to receive letters from my father, I discovered he had quite a way with words. No doubt he employed all his rhetorical skills when writing to my mother, singing Haiyan's praises in the hyperbolic language so often used to describe Hangzhou. She was completely taken in by the honeyed words and bewitching images with which he regaled her. Mistaking the tiny, ramshackle town of Haiyan for a miniature Hangzhou, she decided to forsake life in the provincial capital and reunite us with our father. It must have taken enormous courage to do that, for in that bygone era China's harsh household registration system permitted you to live and work only in a single place, and death alone could free you; you were like a nail that's hammered into a wall, staying there till it rusts and snaps. My mother renounced her Hangzhou residence permit—and Hua Xu's and mine as well—which in those days meant Hangzhou would be lost to us forever. With her two sons in tow she boarded a long-haul bus and traveled down a road of no return.

I was three years old that year, and I am sure that when my mother came out of the bus station in Haiyan, one hand in mine and the other in my brother's, the shock must have been overwhelming. Suddenly she was confronted by the real Haiyan, a very different place from the one she had read about in my father's letters. Later she would often sum up in this way her first reaction to Haiyan's primitive living standards: "You didn't see even a single bicycle!"

Sometimes my mother would wistfully share with us little vignettes from our life in Hangzhou; when she talked of the house where we used to live and the scenery a short walk away, a blissful expression would appear on her face. Such moments would plunge me into endless reverie. Though that brief, idyllic stay in Hangzhou had been erased from my young memory, my mother's reconstruction of it brought it back to life, and during my childhood years it occupied the most beautiful place in my imagination. After every such reminiscence my mother could never stop herself from raising her hand and pointing an accusing finger at my father: "It was you who tricked us into coming to Haiyan!"

These days when my mother recalls the past she puts it differently; time has softened that disappointment and provided a more precise word for the wrong she suffered.

"It was you who bamboozled us into coming here," she says now.

The word "bamboozle," then, has rapidly gained acceptance in China. Just as "copycat" gives imitation and piracy a new range of connotations, "bamboozle" throws a cloak of respectability over deception and manufactured rumor.

In 2008, just a couple of weeks before the opening of the Beijing Olympics, a local newspaper dropped a bombshell. It began:

> Beijing this August will be the most exciting place in the world. Not only will the most outstanding athletes in the world gather here; the rich and powerful of the world believe that visiting Beijing for the Olympics is the ultimate in fashion and have made their bookings months in advance. They include Bill Gates, the world's richest man. However, this software giant—who has already given away billions of dollars to charity—will not be staying at a hotel in Beijing this time. Rather, he has chosen a penthouse apartment less than two hundred yards from the Water Cube. If he opens the windows and looks out, he will get a perfect view of the crystal-blue Water Cube Aquatics Center and the stunning Bird's Nest Stadium.

Bill Gates, we were told, had shelled out a hundred million yuan on his penthouse lease. The report went on:

> The apartment is on two floors and has about 7,500 square feet of space. However, even if you are as rich as Bill Gates, you won't be able to buy it, for these properties are for lease only. Bill Gates has it only on a one-year term, though that will cost a hundred million yuan. "We don't do short-term rentals," sales associate Miss Yi explained.

The article took the form of an interview with this saleslady. After gleefully reporting what a big spender Bill Gates was, Miss Yi waxed even more lyrical as she enthused about the grace and luxury of this new residential complex: "The whole structure resembles a huge jade dragon with head raised and wings extended, its posture magnificent, its spirit lively, and all in perfect accordance with the principles of feng shui." The report added a mysterious touch: apparently it was only "under the guidance of a master" that the building design was elevated to such a high level, with such rich symbolic significance.

"By all accounts, many clients of substance have already put their names down," the article continued to bamboozle.

> "Bill Gates has paid his lease," Miss Yi told us, "and others—I can't reveal their names—have already moved in." Miss Yi, normally so discreet, revealed inadvertently that not all the units had been spoken for. "Some are still unclaimed, and if you want to take out a lease, there is still a chance." When a reporter asked whether one could lease an apartment next to Bill Gates, Miss Yi replied, "It's possible. But first you need to fax over your details and get things verified before we can set up a tour. As to whether or not you can be Mr. Gates' neighbor, you need to complete the first steps before we can discuss that."

As soon as the news got out, China's mainstream and not-so-mainstream media circulated the report, and I think at a minimum more than a hundred million people must have learned about this new residential complex in Beijing. Soon the news spread to the United States, and the Bill & Melinda Gates Foundation issued a formal denial. A few days later Zheng Yaqin, director of Microsoft's China operations, suggested at a press conference that it was simply promotional hype cooked up by a property developer, using the Olympics and Bill Gates to get attention.

When pressed by journalists, the developer denied all responsibility for the article, claiming that it was a fiction concocted by the media. The first media outlet to report the news countered that they got the story directly from the sales associate, Miss Yi. As the pot called the kettle black, people soon stopped caring about where the rumor originated. Even though the media continued to report it as genuine news, none of it made any sense: if Bill Gates spent a hundred million yuan to lease this penthouse, then each square foot would have to cost 13,000 yuan—an absurd figure, for if one were to flat-out purchase the apartment, 5,000 yuan per square foot would be about the going rate. Once people worked this out, the media quickly changed their story, hailing the whole episode as "the supreme bamboozle of 2008."

The media in China today are full of fake stories like this, because there are seldom any legal repercussions. To circulate this kind of story is a kind of fraud, but in China people just shrug it off as bamboozle. In this particular case "bamboozle" implied both deception and hype, but it also contained a certain element of entertainment. That being so, nobody was inclined to regard it as a serious issue.

One thing we did learn, however, was just how much leverage a bamboozle can exert: by playing the Beijing Olympics and Bill Gates for all they were worth, it was able overnight to convert an obscure housing development into an apartment complex famous all over the country. In economic terms, leverage is a monetary policy, confined to profit-and-loss risk management issues; in capital markets it simply makes it possible to clinch large deals with a relatively small outlay—as the Chinese expression goes, "using four ounces to shift a thousand pounds," or as Archimedes said, "Give me a place to stand and I will move the world."

But now we clever Chinese have found a place for leverage in common and everyday bamboozling. Bamboozling is everywhere, and so leverage is everywhere, too.

Chinese authors and publishers, for example, like to use Hollywood as leverage to bamboozle readers and the media. A few years ago one Chinese novel was no sooner published than it was hyped to the skies in the Chinese media. Although the English edition had yet to appear, it was widely touted that Hollywood was going to make a movie out of it, at a price tag of $300 million. As I was puzzling over this, thinking I'd never heard of a Hollywood movie costing so much, the bamboozle industry was upping the ante to $800 million. Aided by this kind of hype, two Chinese novels have indeed become best sellers in recent years, each claiming to be bound for Hollywood at a cost of $800 million. The novel that claimed to be worth a measly $300 million did not sell so well, I think perhaps because it did not employ bamboozle leverage to best effect and failed to "use four ounces to shift a thousand pounds"—its four ounces shifted only four hundred pounds. If you're going to bamboozle at all, then clearly the bigger the better. As we Chinese say, you don't have to pay tax on bullshit. That being so, why not bullshit to the max?

"The more boldly a man dares, the more richly his land bears"—that famous Great Leap Forward mantra—turns out to be an apt description of bamboozlement's essential nature. Its logic is confirmed by another Chinese homily: "The timid die of hunger, the bold of overeating."

Let's now review another case, one in which an entrepreneur used CCTV as leverage to bamboozle others into making him rich. This episode dates back almost twenty years, to a time when China had yet to enter the Internet age but was already a nation overflowing with advertisements. Today, of course, TV commercials and newspaper ads are even more abundant and of infinite variety—imported and domestic, refined and vulgar, violent and erotic. Established companies hawk their wares in neon lights and on expressway billboards; shady, underground businesses paste flyers on utility poles and the steps of pedestrian bridges. Advertising is now so ubiquitous and ostentatious that the big-character posters of the Cultural Revolution years seem tame by comparison.

At the time of this episode, the most expensive advertising spot was a five-second placement before CCTV's *Network News* at seven o'clock each evening. CCTV had begun selling the spot off to the highest bidder, but it was all still in an experimental stage, before the network started to check the financial resources of the bidders. In those days, if a beggar were to dress up in a suit and put a millionaire's smile on his face, there would have been nothing to stop him from going in and making an offer. Whatever company made the highest bid would immediately be hailed as the Bidding King by media outlets big and small, and all this publicity would be even more effective than the five-second commercial itself.

Our entrepreneur had only limited financial resources, and he felt that if he simply continued to do business on a modest scale, he could never hope to be more than a small-timer, even if he pulled out all the stops. Now he saw his opportunity. Like so many other grassroots entrepreneurs in China, once he had set his sights on his goal, he would stop at nothing to reach it. He traveled alone to Beijing and adopted a low-key stance as he entered the CCTV commercial Bidding King auction room, which was thronged with millionaire entrepreneurs and powerful managers of state-owned enterprises. He found a chair in the back row; when the auction began, he sat with head bowed and eyes half closed, as though about to nod off, but every time he heard a bid, he would lift his right hand and make a better offer. As the price rose higher and higher and other companies gradually withdrew from the competition, he kept raising his hand, as cool as a cucumber. In the end he claimed the CCTV Bidding King's crown with an astronomical offer of 80 million yuan.

With this title under his belt our hero returned to his home base and made an appointment to meet with the mayor and the party secretary of the municipal committee. "I've brought back the 80 million yuan Bidding King title for our city," he told them with a winning smile, "but my own assets are just a tiny fraction of that. What shall we do? If you back me up, then our city will have produced an entrepreneur famous throughout the nation. If you let me down, then our city will have produced the biggest trickster in the whole country." He left them with a parting shot of "Do whatever you think is best."

Local officials were then single-mindedly pursuing GDP growth, hoping that the areas under their jurisdiction would produce a nationally known entrepreneur—an achievement they could bandy about as a way of boosting their own chances of promotion. If the most brazen swindler in China were to emerge on their watch, conversely, this would have grim implications for their career prospects. An emergency meeting was called, and after much soul-searching the mayor and the party secretary decided to instruct the local commercial bank to give the Bidding King a loan of 200 million yuan—a loan rich in Chinese flavor, for commercial banks were often then at the beck and call of the local government.

That was how this small-time businessman twice bamboozled his way to success, first by exploiting the leverage offered by CCTV's Bidding King title, then by making the most of Chinese officials' vanity to end up with a nice little haul of 200 million yuan. But his bamboozling wasn't over, for he would then bamboozle himself a reputation as a nationally known entrepreneur.

Stories of this kind keep coming so thick and fast I need to tell a few more: first, two about how people bamboozle the government, then two about how the government bamboozles the people.

Average Chinese citizens have no ambition to be famous and powerful, nor do they dream of making their fortunes overnight; for them contentment brings happiness. So when they bamboozle the government, the leverage effect is that of four ounces lifting four pounds; as long as they enjoy a fair degree of success, they feel pleased with a job well done. Whatever bamboozling leverage they have tends to be found close to home: lacking friends or relatives in high places, lacking access to a wide social network, all they really have in life is family and marriage, so these provide the only real leverage, as the first two stories will show.

Three or four years ago, a city education bureau announced a new measure to raise the quality of local teachers and enable graduating high school seniors to be more competitive in the university entrance examination. All high school teachers were to take part in an examination that would test their credentials. Those who passed could continue teaching; those who failed would have their jobs terminated. At the same time, out of humanitarian considerations, the education bureau noted that some teachers were raising children alone after divorce or the loss of a spouse and might be suffering hardship through the combination of workload and child-care responsibilities, so they issued an additional proviso that the requirement would be waived for teachers who were raising children single-handedly.

It is only since my own son entered middle school that I have realized the crushing weight of examinations in China's educational system. Practically every day he has to prepare for an exam, whether it is a daily exercise or review quiz, or a test, monthly exam, midterm exam, or final exam. There are all manner of tests in Chinese high schools, and from the day they enter the school gates, students are trained to become test-taking machines. But those teachers who were used to testing students daily found a test suddenly staring them in the face, and it made them quake.

The teachers in this small-scale city thereupon began a large-scale bamboozle. The ruling that widowed and divorced teachers with children would be excused from taking the examination gave them just the leverage they needed. Off they rushed to the registry office and filed for divorce. Observing this flood of divorces (and subsequent flood of remarriages), the townsfolk found much to admire. "That's the wisdom of the masses in action," they would tell one another.

Wherever they met, whether in the street or in the school, the teachers soon got in the habit of greeting each other in a new way: "Divorced yet?" Before long, that became a standard greeting all over town. In the end fewer than 30 percent of the teachers took the examination, and most of those were unmarried or married without children; naturally there were a few others too who were confident enough about passing to actually sit for the exam. With the crisis over, remarriages commenced and greetings were revised accordingly: "Remarried yet?"

In the second story, people again leveraged marriage to bamboozle the government, but this time in the countryside—an increasingly common practice there since urbanization quickened its pace. China's long-standing household registration system strictly regulates urban and rural registration. With the rapid growth of China's cities since the 1980s, huge swathes of land surrounding the cities have been requisitioned by the government, with the result that peasant registrations are reclassified, the so-called rural-to-urban shift. Peasants lose their ancestral homes as well as their land, and in compensation the government moves the displaced peasants into newly built urban housing. Just how much square footage each transferred peasants should get involves a complex computation that takes into account the size of their original house and the number of their family members, but marital status is the most crucial element. Marriage and divorce, remarriage and redivorce, thus become the instruments of deception and subterfuge.

A few years ago, when the land of peasants in a township in southwest China was requisitioned, in order to gain maximum advantage and claim the largest possible compensation when new housing was allocated, almost 95 percent of households went through the motions of divorce and then set themselves up with bogus new marriage partners. The marriage registration office was swamped with applications and had to deal with more paperwork in the space of a few months than it would normally handle in years.

Bizarre turns of event added spice to this collective con. An old lady no longer steady on her feet suddenly hit the romantic jackpot, carried off to the registry office on the shoulders of three different young men, to pick up three different marriage licenses. One man went through with the fake divorce quite happily but then balked at the prospect of remarrying his ex-wife. After much stalling and procrastination, he finally told her the truth. "I wanted to end our marriage ages ago," he said, "and now at last I had the chance to bamboozle you into divorce." An old granddad had a phony marriage with a much younger wife and later refused to divorce her. No matter how she wept and pleaded, and even though she promised a severance package, he remained obdurate. Family and friends tried to talk sense into him. "It's just a charade," they reminded him. "How can you take it as real?"

His response was heartfelt: "But for me it was love at first sight!"

As the people con the government, so the government cons the people. As China has transmuted itself from a command economy to a market economy during the past thirty years, some local governments have demonstrated their allegiance to the new order by vigorously promoting auction sales of one kind or another. For instance, they might hold a public auction to sell off the rights to name roads, bridges, squares, residential communities, and high-rise buildings, and whichever company made the highest offer would be free to name a place as it saw fit. In 2006, when one city decided to put up place-names for auction, the announcement elicited some furious reactions from the locals.

"If place-names are up for grabs," some said, "how will people keep track of what's what and where's where?"

"Is our housing complex going to be renamed Ladies' Soother Estates?" others asked sarcastically, referring to the leading brand of vaginal cream.

"When I want to send a letter to my friend, will I have to write the address as Brain Ambrosia Boulevard?" another inquired, alluding to a well-known herbal tonic.

Some took things to their logical extreme, suggesting they might as well put the name of the city itself up for sale—that way they might be able to strike a deal with the Coca-Cola Company and rename the city Coca-Colaville.

Officials rushed to backpedal: "Paid use of place-names is just an idea, and it has yet to be implemented; residents have no cause for alarm. Even if such a system is introduced in the future, it will comply with relevant laws; naming of places will be carefully regulated."

Given the pressure of public opinion, the place-name auction never got off the ground. But when local officials mention this initiative, they applaud it heartily, declaring

that now is the era of the market economy and so things
should be done according to market principles; marketable
operations are the way to go. These past few years, "marketable operation" has become the mantra of local government
officials; sometimes it has given local governments leverage to bamboozle the people. The following two stories are
examples of this trend.

The first story took place in Sichuan Province, in the
city of Neijiang. There the city management bureau was
keen to strengthen its oversight of itinerant vendors, with a
view, no doubt, to increasing its revenues, so it announced
it would auction off its sidewalks. Now, sidewalks are originally designed to provide foot passage; if they are auctioned
off to vendors, they will simply end up carpeted with merchandise, and where will that leave pedestrians? Are pedestrians just going to have to take their lives in their hands
and try their luck among the throngs of cars and trucks and
buses? When I indignantly reported this development to
an official, he shrugged off my concern and told me I was
overreacting. He saw nothing absurd about what they were
doing. "You'll find lots of places where sidewalks are being
auctioned off," he told me.

The second story comes to us from the city of Xiangtan,
in Hunan. There the municipal government announced
that street numbers could be purchased. Chinese people
have a superstitious faith in certain numbers, believing that
the number six, for example, promises a happy outcome and
that eight signifies fortune and prosperity. Residents eagerly
splurged on numbers such as 6, 66, 666, and 6666 and 8, 88,
888, and 8888; as a result, street numbering in some neigh-
borhoods went haywire as regular sequences of numbers
broke down. In a street that originally had odd numbers on
the left and even numbers on the right, when one walked
down the left-hand side of the street, one might no longer
find No. 5 between No. 3 and No. 7, but No. 8888. Or when

one proceeded along the right-hand side, one might very well find No. 6 sandwiched between No. 792 and No. 796. If I were to walk along that street, I wouldn't know whether to laugh or cry.

When sidewalks were auctioned off and auspicious street numbers were sold to the highest bidder, the people of Neijiang and Xiangtan may have cursed for all they were worth, but the local officials just went on talking big, bamboozling them with that regular refrain, "This is how marketable operation works."

All this gives me the sensation that we are living in a fantastic fictional world, in a city called Coca-Colaville whose sidewalks have been taken over by market stalls, where people shuttle nimbly through the gaps left by rapidly moving vehicles like characters in a kung fu movie. Landmarks are differentiated with incongruous names like Black Sister Toothpaste Street, Sixth Sense Condom Bridge, Sanlu Milk Powder Square, and AB Underwear District—every brand in China leaving its mark on the city landscape, from things you eat and wear and use, to furniture and automobiles, lovemaking accessories and paraphernalia for new parents. Street numbers are in random order; every venture down an avenue is like a walk in a labyrinth. Here, where everything is tinged with the mysterious logic of absurdist fiction, Kafka or Borges might feel quite at home. Perhaps one day I'll write such a story myself. *Bamboozletown* might be its title.

There is really no end to these stories of fraud and chicanery, for "bamboozle" has already insinuated itself into every aspect of our lives. If a foreign leader visits China, people will say he's "come to bamboozle," and if a Chinese leader travels abroad, people will say he's "gone to bamboozle those foreigners." When a businessman heads out to negotiate a deal, he'll say he's "off to bamboozle," and when a professor goes to deliver a lecture, he'll say the same thing. Social interactions and romantic partnerships fall under this heading, too: "I bamboozled him into being my friend," you might hear someone say, or "I bamboozled her into falling for me." Even Zhao Benshan, the godfather of bamboozling, has become its casualty. A couple of years ago a text message appeared on many millions of Chinese cell phones:

> Got access to a television? Be sure to turn on CCTV— Zhao Benshan has been killed by a bomb, and the police have sealed off the Northeast. 19 people dead, 11 missing, 1 bamboozled!

The one bamboozled, of course, was the person reading the message.

A friend and I once traveled together to a speaking engagement. Last thing at night he asked me for a couple of sleeping pills. He wasn't planning to take them, he said, but simply to place them next to his bed as a form of subliminal tranquilizer. "They'll bamboozle me into falling asleep," he said with a laugh.

Bamboozlement can also give a new gloss to literary works. There's a famous line by the Tang poet Li Bai: "White hair falling thirty thousand feet." It used to be seen as the quintessence of the Chinese literary imagination, but people's commentary now takes a different form. "That Li Bai sure knew how to bamboozle," they scoff.

Bamboozling has practically become an essential fashion accessory. In the last couple of years schoolchildren have developed a new fad: buying so-called bamboozle cards, which are the same size as drivers' licenses. You see vendors hawking them on city streets and pedestrian bridges: "Bamboozle cards—one yuan each! With bamboozle card in hand or purse, bamboozle the world for all it's worth!"

"Hereby it is certified," the cards read, "that Comrade

So-and-so possesses distinctive technique and rich experience in bamboozling; few are they who can avoid being duped." The bamboozle card is embossed with a round, official-looking stamp just like other Chinese identity cards; its issuing authority is the National Bamboozle Commission. Schoolchildren greet each other by pulling out their cards and waving them in each other's faces, like FBI agents flashing their ID in a Hollywood movie—the ultimate in school-age cool.

The rapid rise in popularity of the word "bamboozle," like that of "copycat," demonstrates to me a breakdown of social morality and a confusion in the value system in China today; it is an aftereffect of our uneven development these past thirty years. If anything, bamboozling is even more widespread in social terms than the copycat phenomenon, and when bamboozling gains such wide acceptance, it goes to show that we live in a frivolous society, one that doesn't set much store by matters of principle.

My concern is that when bamboozling unabashedly becomes a way of life, then everyone from the individual to the population at large can become its victim. For a bamboozler is quite likely to end up bamboozling himself or—in Chinese parlance—to pick up a big stone only to drop it on his own foot.

I imagine everyone has probably had this kind of experience: you try to bamboozle someone, only to end up bamboozling yourself. I am certainly no exception, for when I look back at my own career, I find many such examples. What follows is one such case.

If I remember correctly, my father was the target of my first scam. When I didn't want to do something he wanted me to do, or if he was about to punish me for doing something I shouldn't have done, I often resorted to my own form of leverage: feigned illness. It would have been called deception then, but now we'd call it bamboozling.

It's in every child's nature, I daresay, to try to deceive or bamboozle his or her parents. I was in elementary school by then and aware that there was something wonderful about my relationship with my father. We were kith and kin, in other words, and even if I did something outrageous, I would be unlikely to suffer fatal consequences. I have forgotten exactly what led me to feign illness that first time; all I know is that I was anticipating some form of punishment, and I wanted if at all possible to avoid it. Pretending to be racked by fever, I shuffled with faltering steps toward my incensed father.

After listening to my tale of woe, my father reacted instinctively: he reached out a hand and planted it on my forehead. Only then did I realize what a colossal mistake I had made—I'd forgotten that he was a doctor. Now I'm in for it, I thought: not only would I not escape punishment for my original misdemeanor, but I would surely incur further punishment for this new offense.

Miraculously, my bamboozle managed to slip in under the wire. When my father's discerning hand established that I didn't have the slightest temperature, it didn't seem to occur to him that I was trying to pull the wool over his eyes. He simply expressed outrage that I had not engaged in any healthy exercise that day. I received a stern dressing-down: no longer would I be permitted to loll about the house— I needed to run around outside, even if it was just to get a bit of sun. There was absolutely nothing wrong with me, my father declared; my only problem was that I was so averse to activity. Then he told me to get out of the house. I could do whatever I pleased, but I was not to show my face again for at least two hours.

Out of concern for my health my father's anger had suddenly changed direction, making him forget my transgression of a few minutes earlier and the punishment he originally had planned for me, and allowing me unexpectedly to get off scot-free. I ran out the door and kept going until I had reached a safe distance; there I stood and reflected tensely on my narrow escape. I must never again pretend to have a fever, I concluded, no matter how desperate the situation.

Thereafter my acting performances revolved more around internal disorders. There was a year or two, for example, when I often pretended to have a stomachache, something I was able to carry off quite convincingly. Because as a child I was very picky about food, I often suffered from constipation, and this helped provide a plausible pretext for my stomachaches. If I did something wrong, I'd feel a stab of pain in my belly as soon as I saw my father's face darkening.

At the beginning I was fully aware that I was simply pretending to be ill, but later it became a conditioned reflex. All it took for me to have a stomachache was for my father to get angry, and soon I found it impossible to work out whether the pain was genuine or imaginary. However, to me that was a minor point; the main thing was my father's reaction, for his anger would at once shift to questions of diet and what I chose to eat or not eat, and he would warn me that if I persisted with my food phobias, I wouldn't just suffer from constipation; my physical growth and intellectual development would be compromised as well. Once again his health concerns made him forget the punishment he should have administered; even if he was now even more furious than before, I accepted his rage with equanimity, knowing it would not result in any disciplinary action.

As time went on I resorted to ruses and subterfuges even more often, no longer feigning illness simply to deflect punishment but also to get out of household chores like sweeping or mopping the floor. Once, however, I was too smart for my own good. When I announced that I had a stomachache, my father clapped his hand on a spot in my midriff. "Is this where it hurts?" he asked. I nodded. "Did the pain start higher up, here in the pit of your stomach?" he asked. Again I nodded. My father continued his line of questioning, trying to establish whether my symptoms corresponded with those of appendicitis, and I simply kept nodding to his every question. Actually, by this point I couldn't tell whether it really hurt or not; it just seemed to me that I felt a pain wherever my father's strong hand pressed, just as surely as I would answer whenever he called my name.

Next thing I knew, my father was carrying me piggyback out the door. I lay slumped over his shoulders, disconcerted by this turn of events and utterly in the dark as to what was going to happen next. It was not until my father entered the hospital surgery that I realized things were not looking at all good. At that point I was in a welter of confusion: my father's look of determination made me feel that I perhaps did have appendicitis, but I was aware that when it all started I was just pretending to be in pain, even if it really did feel a bit sore later when my father's probing hand was pressing down on me. My head was spinning; I had no idea what to do. As my father laid me on the operating table, I managed only a feeble demurral. "It doesn't hurt anymore," I said.

He pinned me down on the operating table, and two nurses fastened my hands and feet with leather grips. Now I began frantically to resist. "It doesn't hurt anymore!" I yelled.

I was hoping they would abort the operation that now seemed imminent, but they paid me not the slightest attention. "I want to go home!" I cried. "Let me go home!"

My mother, the head nurse in surgery at the time, placed a piece of cloth over my face. Through the opening in it I issued a piercing scream, reiterating my objection to surgery. Since my hands and feet were tied down, I could only twist my body back and forth to underscore my refusal. Somewhere above I heard my mother's voice: she was telling me not to shout, warning me I could choke to death if I didn't stop. This frightened me, for I didn't understand how shouting could kill me. No sooner did I stop to ponder this question than I felt the spurt of a pungent anesthetic in my mouth, and I quickly lost consciousness.

When I came to, I was lying on my bed at home. I felt my brother stick his head under my sheet and immediately remove it. "He farted," I heard him yell. "Oh, what an awful stink!" Soon my parents were standing by my bed, chuckling. My appendix had been removed, and the gas I discharged in my semicomatose state signaled the success of the operation and confirmed that I would make a quick recovery.

Many years later I asked my father if, when he opened me up and saw my appendix, it really needed to be removed. "Oh, absolutely," he said. What interested me, of course, was whether my appendix had actually been inflamed or not. But on this point my father's answer was ambiguous: "It did look a little puffy."

"What does that mean?" I wondered. My father admitted that a little puffiness might well have cleared up by itself, even without medication, but at the same time he insisted that surgery had been the best option, because medical opinion at the time held that not only appendixes that looked "a little puffy" should be removed but even completely healthy appendixes ought to go.

I used to think my father was right, but now I see things differently: I think it was a case of reaping what one sows. I had originally been bent on bamboozling my father, but in the end I simply bamboozled myself onto the operating table and under the knife.

ALSO BY

YU HUA

THE SEVENTH DAY

Yang Fei was born on a train as it raced across the Chinese countryside. Lost by his mother, adopted by a young switchman, raised with simplicity and love, he is utterly unprepared for the changes that await him and his country. As a young man, he searches for a place to belong in a nation ceaselessly reinventing itself, but he remains on the edges of society. At forty-one, he meets an unceremonious death, and lacking the money for a burial plot, must roam the afterworld aimlessly. There, over the course of seven days, he encounters the souls of people he's lost. As he retraces the path of his life, we meet an extraordinary cast of characters: his adoptive father, his beautiful ex-wife, his neighbors who perished in the demolition of their homes. Vivid, urgent, and panoramic, Yang Fei's passage movingly traces the contours of his vast nation—its absurdities, its sorrows, and its soul.

Fiction

ALSO AVAILABLE

Boy in the Twilight
Brothers
Chronicle of a Blood Merchant
Cries in the Drizzle
To Live

ANCHOR BOOKS
Available wherever books are sold.
www.anchorbooks.com